TC
31.5.98
[?]ald TH

BRANCH LINES TO EXMOUTH

Vic Mitchell and Keith Smith

MP Middleton Press

First published April 1992

ISBN 1 873793 006

© Middleton Press 1992

Typesetting   - Barbara Mitchell
Design   - Deborah Goodridge

Published by Middleton Press
              Easebourne Lane
              Midhurst
              West Sussex
              GU29 9AZ
              Tel: (0730) 813169

Printed & bound by Biddles Ltd,
              Guildford and Kings Lynn

CONTENTS

INDEX

ACKNOWLEDGEMENTS

In addition to the photographers mentioned in the captions, we have received much assistance from R.M.Casserley, Dr.E.Course, G.Croughton, Mrs.S.Grove, J.Harries, M.King, N.Langridge, A.Ll.Lambert, D.Salter, E.B.Staff, N.Stanyon, A.E.West, R.White, E.S.Youldon and our ever helpful wives. To all these we would like to express our deep gratitude.

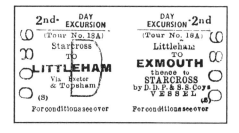

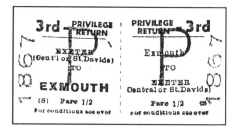

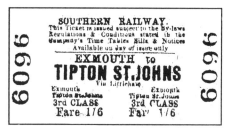

1955 map with Southern Region routes shown with wide lines and Western Region narrow.

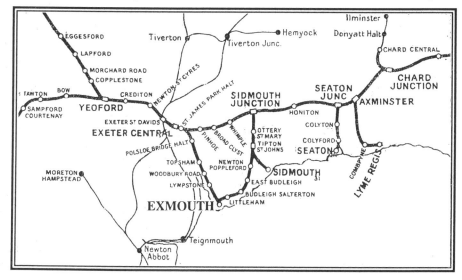

HISTORICAL BACKGROUND

The London & South Western Railway's main line from London reached Exeter (Queen Street) on 19th July 1860. Prior to this, plans had been drawn by Brunel for a broad gauge branch from Exminster to Exmouth and an Act of Parliament was obtained on 2nd July 1855. A massive bridge across the wide River Exe was proposed. No work was undertaken but, on 12th July 1858, an Act was passed to allow the construction of a branch from the planned LSWR main line to Topsham. This opened on 1st May 1861, along with an extension to Exmouth on the route of the proposed broad gauge line, the Exminster-Topsham plan having been abandoned. The LSWR worked the branch from the outset and absorbed it on 29th June 1871.

The second and successful Act for a branch line from Feniton to Sidmouth was passed on 29th June 1871, the railway opening on 6th July 1874.

The Budleigh Salterton Railway was authorised on 20th July 1894 and was opened as a branch from Tipton St.Johns on 15th May 1897. The extension to Exmouth was completed by the LSWR on 1st June 1903.

All the routes became part of the Southern Railway in 1923 and were incorporated into the Southern Region of British Railways in 1948. They were transferred to the Western Region on 1st January 1963, dieselisation following towards the end of the year.

The Sidmouth line and its branch to Exmouth closed to passengers on 6th March 1967.

July 1917

June 1869

PASSENGER SERVICES

	Exeter - Exmouth		Tipton St.Johns - Exmouth	
	Weekdays	Sundays	Weekdays	Sundays
1908	18	6	10	-
1917	12	4	5	-
1924	20	7	10	-
1928	21	12	13	6
1937	27	19	12	6
1944	19	11	9	-
1948	23	13	12	4
1954	24	13	10	4
1962	32	17	11	5
1966	26	9	8	6
1974	20	12	-	-
1986	28	13	-	-

Exeter-Exmouth

The first timetable showed five trains daily. The weekday frequency increased to 7 in 1863, 10 in 1881, and 11 by 1890. The Sunday service remained at about five journeys until 1922.

The table above indicates the changing pattern of services but omits trains running on certain days only and those making short journeys. For example, between about 1908 and 1915 there were nine trips daily by steam railcar between Exeter and Topsham. The frequency shown is for down trains in the summer period. A feature of Sunday travel between the wars was the operation of National Sunday League excursions from Waterloo and from Christchurch.

A through train was run from Exmouth to Manchester via Exeter St.Davids from 1949 until 1967. This summer Saturdays service was not advertised as a through running until 1963.

Unusual local workings included one or two extra trains from Exmouth to Exeter at nearly midnight, in connection with combined admission tickets to the Pavilion Ballroom.

These trains ran on Saturday nights only from 1948 until 1968.

Until 1986, only a few peak hour trains failed to call at all stations but thereafter there were several limited stop trains during the day, the service having been improved considerably from May of that year.

Winter Sunday trains were withdrawn for most of the 1970s.

Tipton St.Johns-Exmouth

Initially, the Tipton St.Johns-Budleigh Salterton service comprised eight trains each way, weekdays only. A similar service was maintained after the extension to Exmouth, although there were some additional short workings.

Through coaches from Waterloo were a useful feature from the early years, an Exmouth portion being included in Britain's most multi-portioned train, the "Atlantic Coast Express". Entire trains were run through from Waterloo between the wars and in most post war years until 1965.

In the 1930s, there was a through train from Nottingham via the Somerset & Dorset line at peak holiday times. Similarly, a service ran over the same route from Cleethorpes in 1960-62.

In most periods some trains on the route originated from Sidmouth or Sidmouth Junction. A few peak hour services originated at Budleigh Salterton and ran through to Exeter Central via Exmouth. In the diesel era some trains operated between Sidmouth and Exeter, necessitating reversals at Tipton St. Johns and Exmouth.

Sunday services in winter ceased in the final decades.

October 1881

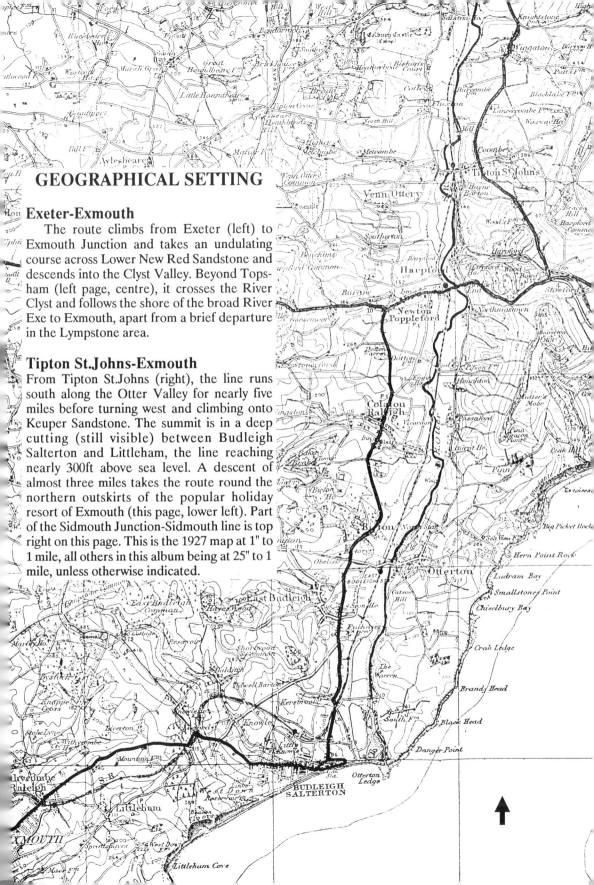

GEOGRAPHICAL SETTING

Exeter-Exmouth

The route climbs from Exeter (left) to Exmouth Junction and takes an undulating course across Lower New Red Sandstone and descends into the Clyst Valley. Beyond Topsham (left page, centre), it crosses the River Clyst and follows the shore of the broad River Exe to Exmouth, apart from a brief departure in the Lympstone area.

Tipton St.Johns-Exmouth

From Tipton St.Johns (right), the line runs south along the Otter Valley for nearly five miles before turning west and climbing onto Keuper Sandstone. The summit is in a deep cutting (still visible) between Budleigh Salterton and Littleham, the line reaching nearly 300ft above sea level. A descent of almost three miles takes the route round the northern outskirts of the popular holiday resort of Exmouth (this page, lower left). Part of the Sidmouth Junction-Sidmouth line is top right on this page. This is the 1927 map at 1" to 1 mile, all others in this album being at 25" to 1 mile, unless otherwise indicated.

1. Tipton St.Johns to Littleham

TIPTON ST.JOHNS

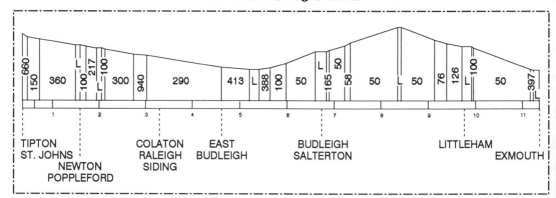

TIPTON ST. JOHNS		COLATON RALEIGH SIDING		EAST BUDLEIGH		BUDLEIGH SALTERTON			LITTLEHAM		EXMOUTH
NEWTON POPPLEFORD											

1. A new 33-lever signal box came into use in March 1897, prior to the opening of the branch, when a run round loop was also added in the goods yard. The white wicket gate allowed pedestrians to cross the line when the main gates were across the road. The wickets were locked just before the arrival of the train. (Lens of Sutton)

The 1890 survey indicates the arrangement prior to the station becoming the junction for Budleigh Salterton on 15th May 1897. Confusion with Tipton (Staffs.) resulted in "St.Johns" being added to the name on 1st February 1881.

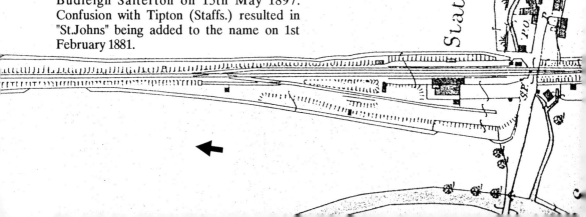

2. The driver oils up prior to departure with his class O2 on 18th June 1926. The footbridge in the background was required by the Board of Trade when the station became a junction. (H.C.Casserley)

3. Seen on 15th June 1949, class M7 no.49 leaves with the 9.42am to Exmouth, which had been the rear portion of the 9.26 from Sidmouth Junction. The Sidmouth portion had left at 9.40. The next photograph shows that the down branch points were moved further south. This was carried out in 1954. (S.C.Nash)

4. A glimpse from the window of a Sidmouth-bound train on 4th May 1957 shows its route climbing steeply at 1 in 45, while the Budleigh Salterton line curves to the right. The footbridge lost its roof in the mid-1950s. (A.E.Bennett)

5. In the 1950s, cheap holidays could be had in redundant coaches at various country stations. By the summer of 1961 ex-Pullman accommodation was on offer and the "camping coach" had become the "holiday coach". (Wessex coll.)

6. Youthful admirers watch class 4 no. 2-6-4T no. 80036 clank into the down platform with an Exmouth train, as a DMU waits in the goods loop to form a connecting service in the summer of 1963. The up signal is mounted on a concrete post.
(J.W.T.House/C.L.Caddy coll.)

7. An A40 rumbles over the crossing as ex-LMS class 2 no. 41206 stands in the down platform on 7th March 1965. A stream passes under the level crossing, giving a convenient source of water for the tank on the left. The gates were operated by a wheel in the signal box. (Wessex coll.)

Summer Saturday timetable for 1962.

Down														Until 25th August Through Carriages from Waterloo dep 8 3 am (Table 35)		Through Carriages from Waterloo dep. 9 0 am (Table 35)	
Saturdays																	
	am	am	am	am	am	am	am	am	am	am	am		am		am		pm
Sidmouth Junction dep	6 30	..	..	8 5	8 31	..	..	9 22	..	1045	1112	..		1142		1 9
Ottery St. Mary	6 37	..	..	8 12	8 36	..	..	9 27	..	1050	1120	..		1149		1 16
Tipton St. John's arr	6 42	..	..	8 17	8 41	..	..	9 32	..	1055	1128	..		1155		1 22
Tipton St. John's dep	6 43	..	..	8 18	8 43	..	..	9 40	..	1028	1056	1130		1157		1 25
Sidmouth arr	6·53	..	..	8 27	8 52	..	..	9 50	..	1036	11 5	1140		12 7		1 35
Tipton St. John's dep	..	..	7 38	..	..	8 48	..	..	..	..	..	1138		12 4		1 31
Newton Poppleford	..	..	7 41	..	..	8 51	..	..	..	..	..	1141		12 9		1 36
East Budleigh	..	..	7 46	..	..	8 56	..	..	..	..	..	1146		1215		1 41
Budleigh Salterton arr	..	..	7 50	..	..	9 0	..	..	..	..	..	1150		1222		1 47
Budleigh Salterton dep	..	6 55	7 51	..	..	9 1	..	1025	..	..	..	1151		1225		1 48
Littleham	..	7 2	7 58	..	..	9 7	..	1032	..	..	..	1157		1234		1 55
Exmouth arr	..	7 10	8 4	..	..	9 12	..	1037	..	..	..	12 2		1240		2 2

Down			Through Carriages from Waterloo dep 11 45 am (Table 35)				28th July to 1st Sept. Through Train from Cleethorpes (Tables 18a, 35 and 36)										
Saturdays—continued																	
	pm	pm		pm	pm	pm		pm	pm	pm	pm	pm	pm	pm	pm	pm	pm
Sidmouth Junction dep	1 55	..		3 2	3 53	..		4 54	5 18	..	..	6 22	7 23	..	8 30	..	9 47	..
Ottery St. Mary	2 0	..		3 9	3 58	..		5 0	5 23	..	..	6 27	7 28	..	8 35	..	9 52	..
Tipton St. John's arr	2 5	..		3 14	4 3	..		5 5	5 28	..	..	6 32	7 33	..	8 40	..	9 57	..
Tipton St. John's dep	2 7	..		3 16	4 5	..		5 7	5 29	..	..	6 34	7 34	8 0	8 42	..	9 58	..
Sidmouth arr	2 16	..		3 26	4 15	..		5 17	5 38	..	..	6 44	7 43	8 8	8 51	..	10 7	..
Tipton St. John's dep	..	2 22		3 22	..	4 45		..	5 12	..	5 50	6 40	..	..	8 47	..	10 5
Newton Poppleford	..	2 25		3 27	..	4 48		..	..	5 53	6 44	..	..	8 50	..	10 8
East Budleigh	..	2 30		3 34	..	4 53		5 20	5 58	6 49	8 55	1014
Budleigh Salterton arr	..	2 34		3 40	..	4 57		5 26	6 2	6 54	8 59	1020
Budleigh Salterton dep	..	2 34		3 42	..	4 58		5 27	6 2	6 55	9 0	1021
Littleham	..	2 42		3 51	..	5 6		5 35	6 10	6 43	7 3	9 7	1028
Exmouth arr	..	2 46		3 58	..	5 11		5 40	6 15	6 48	7 8	9 12	1033

> **Other views and a later map of this station can be found in our** *Branch Lines to Seaton & Sidmouth.*

8. The introduction of DMUs in 1963 brought greater operating flexibility and connecting opportunities at this station. Pictured on 13th September 1966 are contrasting styles of unit. On the left is the 16.45 Sidmouth to Exmouth waiting to reverse, while the 16.45 Sidmouth Junction to Sidmouth stands on the right. (J.M.Tolson/F.Hornby)

9. Track recovery commenced on 28th May 1968 at Sidmouth Junction but was interrupted by severe flooding of the River Otter on 10th July. This is a southward view towards Newton Poppleford, four days later. (S.P.Derek)

2nd **SINGLE SINGLE** 2nd

RAIL MOTOR CAR

Newton Poppleford to

(E.M)   (E.M)

OTTERY ST. MARY

(S)   8d FARE 8d   (S)

For conditions see over For conditions see over

0347   0347

SOUTHERN RAILWAY.

This Ticket is issued subject to the By-laws Regulations & Conditions stated in the Company's Time Tables Bills & Notices
Available on DAY of issue ONLY

NEWTON POPPLEFORD to

N.Poppleford   N.Poppleford
Tipton St.Johns   Tipton St.Johns

TIPTON ST.JOHNS

Third Class   Third Class
Fare 2½d   Fare 2½d

2984   2984

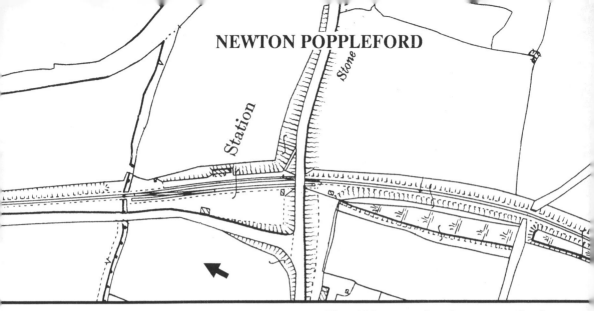

NEWTON POPPLEFORD

Station

Stone

Newton Poppleford	1928	1936
No. of passenger tickets issued	7856	4306
No. of season tickets issued	41	48
No. of tickets collected	5744	3919
Parcels forwarded	580	594
Parcels received	598	1102
General goods forwarded (tons)	169	70
General goods received (tons)	873	728
Coal, Coke etc.	620	940
Other minerals received	297	45
Trucks livestock forwarded	9	3
Trucks livestock received	-	1
Lavatory pennies	-	240

The 1905 map marks a footway running from the south end of the platform up to the road.

2nd **SINGLE**		SINGLE - **2nd**
3435	**Tipton St. Johns** to Tipton St. Johns · Newton P'ford · Tipton St. Johns · Newton P'ford **NEWTON POPPLEFORD** (S) 4d. **FARE** 4d. (S) For conditions see over · For conditions see over	3435

10. The single siding passed under the road bridge (right) and provided an ideal location for camping coaches. In the summer of 1949 nos. 3 and 11 (ex-LCDR nos. 1675 and 1764) were sent to this peaceful location, close to the River Otter. (S.C.Nash)

CAMPING COACH

11. The crossing on the left gave convenient barrow access to the north end of the platform, which was remote from the highway. Class 3 2-6-2T no. 82013 is bound for Tipton St.Johns in September 1957 and is hauling Maunsell coaches retired from main line use. (T.Wright)

12. The station did not open until 1st June 1899, more than two years after services on the line commenced. New sleepers were in evidence when the small building was photographed in September 1961. Freight facilities were withdrawn on 27th January 1964 and staffing ceased on 16th August 1965. (Wessex coll.)

13. A tiny train spotter symbolises the small passenger figures at this location. Seen in 1963, the station and road bridge were soon to disappear without trace. Only the trees and gateway to the goods yard remain. (J.W.T.House/C.L.Caddy coll.)

Until 1st February 1953 a public goods siding was situated at the end of the lane from Colaton Raleigh and is shown on the 1933 edition. It was nearly two miles south of Newton Poppleford station.

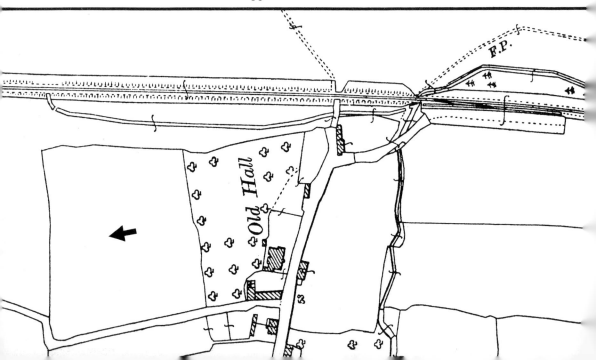

BICTON WOODLAND RAILWAY

14. Two photographs from 1969 show the 18" gauge railway laid out in the garden of Bicton House. Much of the equipment was acquired from the Woolwich Arsenal Railway, the only steam locomotive being no.1 *Woolwich*, an 0-4-0T built by Avonside in 1916. (T.Wright)

15. No.3 *Carnegie*, an 0-4-4-0 diesel mechanical locomotive constructed by Hunslet in 1954, is seen with some of the railway's nine coaches. The line is nearly two miles in length and is open to the public in the holiday season. (T.Wright)

EAST BUDLEIGH

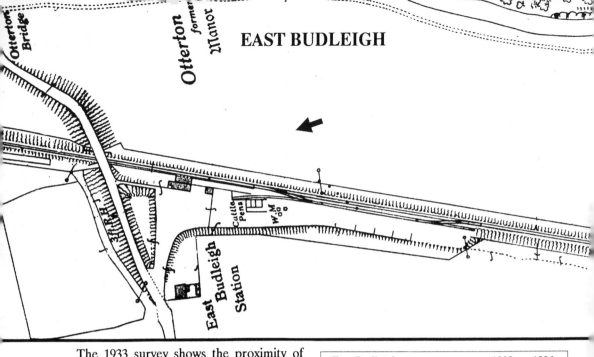

The 1933 survey shows the proximity of Otterton Bridge which is at the west end of the village of Otterton. East Budleigh is about one mile westwards from the station.

16.   The station opened with the line, but the prefix "East" was not added until 27th April 1898. A coal lorry stands in the yard as class O2 0-4-4T no.199 heads the 11.50am Exmouth to Sidmouth service on 16th June 1949. The leading coach would be attached to other coaches for Waterloo at Tipton St.Johns. (S.C.Nash)

East Budleigh	1928	1936
No. of passenger tickets issued	12993	2170
No. of season tickets issued	78	28
No. of tickets collected	18082	3230
No. of telegrams	326	117
Parcels forwarded	921	377
Parcels received	1186	1554
Horses forwarded	-	7
Cans of milk forwarded	635	282
General goods forwarded (tons)	473	232
General goods received (tons)	1100	515
Coal, Coke etc.	1111	1023
Other minerals received	1650	15
Trucks livestock forwarded	82	16
Trucks livestock received	72	11
Lavatory pennies	-	233

17. Standing on timber on 29th June 1948 were camping coaches nos. 11 and 6, originally LCDR five-compartment carriages nos.1764 and 1704. All such holiday dwellings were removed each winter for works servicing. In later years, the coaches stood here on an isolated length of track. (J.H.Aston)

18. The sign mentions nearby Otterton but Ladram Bay is over one mile eastwards and is a popular beach and camping area. A north-bound diesel stops to collect a solitary lady in 1963. The goods closure and destaffing dates are as for Newton Poppleford.
(Lens of Sutton)

19. In addition to the goods shed (left), there was a store for Silcocks' cattle feed in the goods yard. The concrete building is visible in the previous picture. This view is from September 1966, six months before closure. (Wessex coll.)

20. A 1991 view of the west elevation from the public highway shows that a tasteful conversion to a private residence has taken place. The nearby Otterton Mill has been restored to working order and is open to the public. Both preserved buildings enhance the historic locality. (M.Turvey)

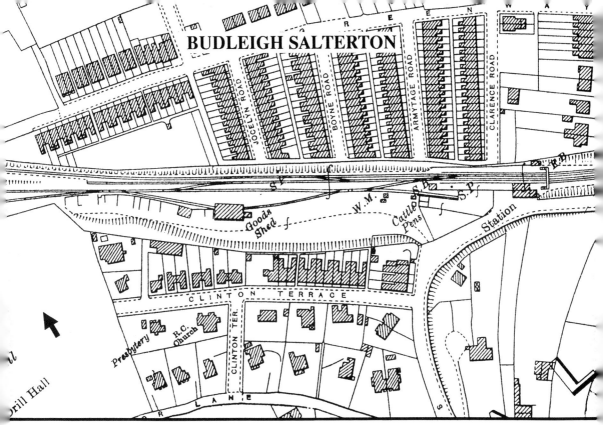

BUDLEIGH SALTERTON

The 1933 survey includes two short sidings on the left. The lower one originally served an engine shed, only 50 x 18ft in size. This housed the branch locomotive and remained in use for some years after the line was extended to Exmouth.

21. The up platform (left) was added prior to the station ceasing to be a terminus in 1903. Trains regularly crossed here thereafter, as witnessed on 22nd May 1957. The coach on the left is one of a batch of BR standard design, built at Swindon from 1956 onwards. (T.Wright)

22.   On the right is evidence of local staff promotional enterprise. Class 3 2-6-2T no. 82019 is about to leave at 10.6am on 18th August 1959, with two coaches for Waterloo and three for Sidmouth. Blowing off is class 2 no.41308, ready to depart for Exmouth at 10.5. (S.P.Derek)

23.   Class 3 no.82025 stands close to the 1903 steel footbridge on 9th July 1959, while working the 6.16pm Exmouth-Budleigh Salterton service. Also evident is the full extent of the goods yard, which closed on 27th January 1964. (R.C.Riley)

Budleigh Salterton	1928	1936
No. of passenger tickets issued	37088	12424
No. of season tickets issued	196	98
No. of tickets collected	55420	19217
No. of telegrams	1227	822
Parcels forwarded	3536	2493
Parcels received	14295	16433
Horses forwarded	27	81
Cans of milk forwarded	296	-
Cans of milk received	118	259
General goods forwarded (tons)	381	226
General goods received (tons)	1840	1291
Coal, Coke etc.	5010	4955
Other minerals forwarded	38	62
Other minerals received	1994	273
Trucks livestock forwarded	6	-
Trucks livestock received	20	1
Lavatory pennies	648	675

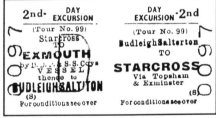

24.   Taken a few minutes after the last photograph, no. 82025 is backing onto the other end of the train in readiness to return to Exmouth at 6.38pm. The train had given a service to business people, having left Exeter Central at 5.45pm. (R.C.Riley)

25. The signal box was similar to that at Lyme Regis and, as at that station, the cattle dock was behind it. In the later years few animals were loaded, but their hides were sent out in large quantities. In the 1950s up to 40,000 tons of stone was received annually from the nearby Black Hill Quarries and despatched to Portishead. (Wessex coll.)

26. The main building, seen six months before closure, was demolished, but the goods shed was incorporated into Norman's Cash & Carry Warehouse. The local population was about 3000 in 1930 and did not exceed 4000 during the life of the line. (Wessex coll.)

THROUGH TRAIN SERVICE

BETWEEN

CLEETHORPES, GRIMSBY, LINCOLN, NOTTINGHAM, LEICESTER, BIRMINGHAM

AND

AXMINSTER (for Lyme Regis), SEATON JUNCTION (for Seaton), SIDMOUTH, BUDLEIGH SALTERTON, EXMOUTH

VIA BATH GREEN PARK AND TEMPLECOMBE

SATURDAYS ONLY

COMMENCES 1st JULY

From NORTH to SOUTH		From SOUTH to NORTH	
	am		am
Cleethorpes .. .. dep	7 0	Exmouth.. .. ..dep	10A42
Grimsby Docks .. .. ,,	7 8	Littleham .. .. ,,	10A47
Grimsby Town .. .. ,,	7 14	Budleigh Salterton .. .. ,,	10A55
Healing .. .. ,,	6b32	East Budleigh .. .. ,,	10 59
Habrough .. .. ,,	7 27	Sidmouth .. .. ,,	11A 7
Barnetby.. .. .. ,,	7 40	Tipton St. Johns .. .. ,,	11 16
Market Rasen .. .. ,,	8 0	Sidmouth Junction .. .. ,,	11 33
Lincoln (St. Mark's) .. .. .. ,,	8 27	Seaton .. .. ,,	11 7
Newark (Castle) .. .. ,,	8 53	Seaton Junction .. .. ,,	11 53
Fiskerton .. .. ,,	9 1	Lyme Regis .. .. ,,	11 8
Nottingham (Mid.) .. .. ,,	9 23		pm
Trent .. .. ,,	9 36	Axminster .. .. ,,	12 1
Loughborough (Mid.) .. .. .. ,,	9 49	Templecombe .. .. ,,	12 48
Leicester London Road .. .. .. ,,	10 10	Evercreech Junction .. .. .. ,,	1 10
Hinckley.. .. .. ,,	10 33	Bath Green Park .. .. ,,	2 18
Nuneaton Abbey Street .. .. .. ,,	10 43		
Birmingham New Street .. .. .. ,,	11 36	Gloucester Eastgate .. .. .. arr	3 16
	pm	Cheltenham Spa (Lansdown) .. .. ,,	4c20
Cheltenham Spa (Lansdown) .. .. ,,	12 47	Birmingham New Street .. .. .. ,,	4 44
Gloucester Eastgate .. .. ,,	1 5	Nuneaton Abbey Street .. .. .. ,,	5 26
		Hinckley.. .. .. ,,	5 37
Bath Green Park .. .. arr	2 2	Leicester London Road .. .. .. ,,	6 0
Evercreech Junction .. .. .. ,,	3 9	Loughborough (Mid.) .. .. .. ,,	6 24
Templecombe .. .. ,,	3 32	Trent .. .. ,,	6 36
Axminster .. .. ,,	4 21	Nottingham (Mid.) .. .. ,,	6 51
Lyme Regis .. .. ,,	5 3	Fiskerton .. .. ,,	7d30
Seaton Junction .. .. ,,	4 29	Newark (Castle) .. .. ,,	7 21
Seaton .. .. ,,	4 57	Lincoln (St. Mark's) .. .. .. ,,	7 53
Sidmouth Junction .. .. .. ,,	4 51	Market Rasen .. .. ,,	8 21
Tipton St. Johns .. .. ,,	5 5	Barnetby.. .. .. ,,	8 44
Sidmouth .. .. ,,	5 17	Habrough .. .. ,,	8 57
East Budleigh .. .. ,,	5 21	Healing .. .. ,,	9 6
Budleigh Salterton .. .. .. ,,	5 26	Grimsby Town .. .. ,,	9 13
Littleham .. .. ,,	5 35	Grimsby Docks .. .. ,,	9 20
Exmouth.. .. .. ,,	5 40	Cleethorpes .. .. ,,	9 31

A—Seats may be reserved at a fee of 2/– per seat upon personal or postal request to the Station Master. Early application is advisable

b—Change at Habrough

c—Change at Gloucester Eastgate

d—Change at Nottingham (Mid.)

July 1961

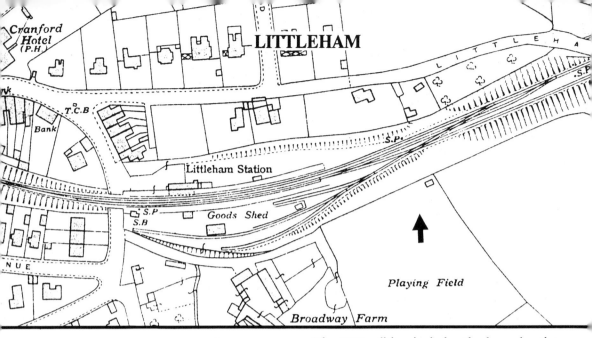

LITTLEHAM

Littleham	1928	1936
No. of passenger tickets issued	14453	3109
No. of season tickets issued	70	25
No. of tickets collected	188443	4363
No. of telegrams.	210	287
Parcels forwarded	559	410
Parcels received	1604	1889
Cans of milk forwarded	-	1149
Cans of milk received	-	553
General goods forwarded (tons)	63	45
General goods received (tons)	483	349
Coal, Coke etc.	1752	649
Other minerals forwarded	537	-
Other minerals received	2141	94
Trucks livestock forwarded	30	16
Trucks livestock received	25	5
Lavatory pennies	180	144

The 1933 edition includes the long shunting neck (right) which was later used for coach berthing, notably the stock of the Saturdays-only Cleethorpes-Exmouth train, for six days a week in the summer. The entire site is now occupied by local authority housing.

27. Features of note in this picture from the LSWR era are the two-tone canopy valance, the wooden goods shed and granite setts in the level crossing. The picture was probably taken soon after the station opened on 1st June 1903 and includes an Adams class 415 4-4-2T. (Lens of Sutton)

28. Another early view shows the east end of the station and the ground frame that controlled access to the goods yard. The station soon attracted building development in its environs, the old village being more than half a mile to the east. (Lens of Sutton)

29. Three camping coaches are evident in the yard on 17th September 1958, as are both the canopies of the goods shed. The ground frame has gone and the point rodding extends to the signal box. The goods yard closed on 27th January 1964. (Pamlin Prints)

30.   The 11.8am Exmouth-Tipton St.Johns freight on 11th March 1961 included camping coaches to be shunted off at East Budleigh for the holiday season. The coaches will have travelled from Eastleigh Works in various goods trains, the final leg of their journey being behind class M7 no.30124. (S.P.Derek)

31.   So that the station could be staffed by one man, a ticket office was built onto the side of the signal box in May 1961. The perfectly matching extension is seen on 19th August 1961, as class 2 no.41284 arrives with empty stock to form the 9.10am Littleham-Waterloo service. This train ran on Saturdays in the summer only. (S.P.Derek)

32. Photographed in March 1965, the structures had changed little during the life of the line, apart from the signal box extension. Partially visible is a board proclaiming *CATCH POINTS*. These were at the top of the incline at 1 in 50 from Exmouth. (C.L.Caddy)

NORTH OF EXMOUTH

33. The late Victorian residents refused to allow the line from Budleigh Salterton to be built through the centre of their town and in consequence this expensive structure was needed to encircle the northern part of the residential area. The picture was taken on 12th October 1959 as class 3 no.82025 descends the steep gradient to Exmouth. (R.C.Riley)

2. Exeter Central to Exmouth

EXETER CENTRAL

The 1888 edition at 6" to 1 mile has the GWR's Exeter St.Davids on the left and below it is the 1862 curve to the LSWR's Exeter Queen Street, which was renamed Exeter Central on 1st July 1933. Lower right is the branch to Exmouth and above it the main line to Yeovil and Waterloo and the 1887 engine shed.

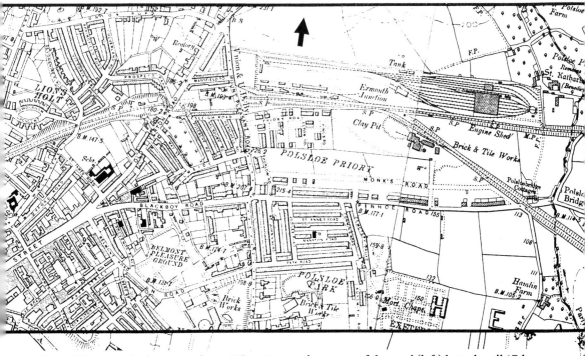

The 1880 survey is shown at about 20" to 1 mile and includes an engine shed which was superseded by the larger one seen on the extreme right of the previous map. The station had separate entrances on opposite sides of the track at that time. The turntables in the southern part of the yard (left) lasted until 17th March 1931 but those north of the line remained in place until 1968. Public freight traffic ceased on 4th December 1967 but cement traffic continued until January 1990, from sidings adjacent to the up platform.

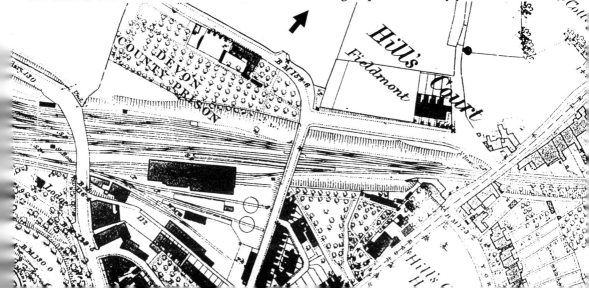

34. Until 1874, there was only one passenger platform (left) and the train shed over two tracks, up trains having to cross to the down line. For many years there was a separate ticket collecting platform between the two road bridges, east of the station. The roof on the right, the up platform and up bay were all added in 1874. The platform extension in the foreground and the crossover date from 1925. These allowed two trains from the west to be accommodated simultaneously and facilitated their combination as a through train to London. (Lens of Sutton)

35. A view from 1930 shows work commencing on the major reconstruction of the station. The down bay (left) was at last given direct connections to the running lines, the gloomy sheds were dismantled, each platform was provided with buffets (until 1971) and a new street-level entrance direct from Queen Street was built. An Exmouth train stands in the up bay which had an engine release crossover at its far end. (Lens of Sutton)

London & South Western Ry.
This Ticket is issued subject to the Regulations & Conditions stated in the Company's Time Tables & Bills

EXETER QUEEN St. to
EXMOUTH

| Queen St. | Queen St. |
| Exmouth | Exmouth |

3rd CLASS (S.38) 3rd CLASS

Fare 10½d   Fare 10½d

3398

SOUTHERN RAILWAY.
This Ticket is issued subject to the By-laws Regulations & Conditions stated in the Company's Time Tables Bills & Notices.
Available on DAY of issue ONLY

EXETER QUEEN St. to

| Exeter Q.St. | Exeter Q.St. |
| MountPleasantH | MountPleasantH |

MOUNT PLEASANT HALT

Third Class   Third Class
Fare 1½d   Fare 1½d

0005

A later map and other views of this station can be seen in our *Yeovil to Exeter* album. The pictures are numbered 100 to 120.

36.   Each of the extended platforms was provided with a long canopy, the down one now being much shortened. The new concrete bridge in the distance linked the platforms to an additional entrance, which had its own passimeter style booking office. This enabled one man to issue and collect tickets. (D.Cullum coll.)

37. Marshalling yards at Exmouth Junction and St.David's sorted the wagons for Exeter Central, transfer being by local trip workings several times a day. Class M7 no.123 is shunting on 20th April 1938. (J.R.W.Kirkby)

SOUTHERN RAILWAY.
This ticket is issued subject to the Company's
Bye-laws, Regulations and Conditions in their
Time Tables, Notices and Book of Regulations.
Available on DAY of issue ONLY.
EXETER QUEEN ST. to
ExeterQ.St.   ExeterQ.St
Polsloe B, H,   Polsloe B, H,
POLSLOE BRIDGE HALT
Third Class   Third Class
Fare 2½d   Fare 2½d
1070

38. Recorded on 30th August 1954 is another M7, no.30676, hauling assorted ex-LSWR coaches forming the 3.45pm from Exmouth. The ticket collecting platform had been sited here earlier. Also included is "A" Box, which was commissioned on 15th June 1927, and the carriage shed which dates from 1930. (J.N.Faulkner)

39. An Exmouth service is departing from the up bay on 29th June 1957, with class O2 no.30232 piloting class 3 no.82017. The coupling of engines was a convenient way to reduce light engine movement. This bay could not be used for Exmouth arrivals after November 1973, as the facing crossover on the main line was taken out then. (R.C.Riley)

THE USE OF THIS CROSSING
BY THE STAFF OF ALL
DEPARTMENTS IS PROHIBITED
UNLESS SPECIALLY AUTHORISED
THE FOOTBRIDGE MUST BE

SOUTHERN RAILWAY
PASSENGERS
MUST NOT CROSS
THE LINE HERE

40. The severity of the gradient up from St.Davids (1 in 37) is evident as the coaches pass the level track of the goods yard on 1st August 1958. No.34034 *Honiton* is displaying the headcode for Exmouth Junction, as it will be running light engine to the shed after detaching the coaches in the platform. On the right is "B" Box, which was in use from 13th September 1925 until 23rd February 1970. (E.W.Fry)

London & South Western Ry.
This Ticket is issued subject to the Regulations & Conditions stated in the Company's Time Tables & Bills

EXETER QUEEN ST. to

EXETER ST. DAVID'S

Queen St.   Queen St.
St. David's   St. David's

3rd CLASS (S.18) 3rd CLASS

Fare 1d   Fare 1d

41. The up through line and the scissors cross-over were taken out of use in 1967-69 and staffing levels reduced drastically. An Exmouth-bound DMU stands at the up platform on 19th November 1983, most such services having originated at St.Davids since 1976. The down through line lasted until October 1984. (P.G.Barnes)

42. The 12.15 from Exmouth enters platform 2 on 27th June 1990, as a Waterloo train climbs the 1 in 100 towards St.James Park. On the right is the line to the bay platform, then only used by three trains a day. The signal box was the last in use at the station, closing on 6th May 1985, when St.Davids panel took control of the area. (P.G.Barnes)

43. City councillors persuaded the SR not to implement their plan to build a replica of Exmouth station here. Instead, this imposing structure was built in 1932-33, and is seen in 1990, by which time only one third of the ground floor of the main building was used for railway purposes. (J.Scrace)

44. The air of dereliction was reduced by the planting of shrubs and operating flexibility was increased by signalling the down line between St.Davids and Central for reversible running. Contrasting DMU vehicles (Metropolitan Cammell and Derby) form the 11.08 Paignton to Exmouth on 12th October 1990 - some trains for the branch originated at Barnstaple. (D.Wilson)

ST. JAMES PARK

45. Opened as Lions Holt Halt on 26th January 1906, the name was changed on 7th October 1946 to emphasise its proximity to the local football ground. Before improvements in bus services, the halt was much used by local residents. (British Rail)

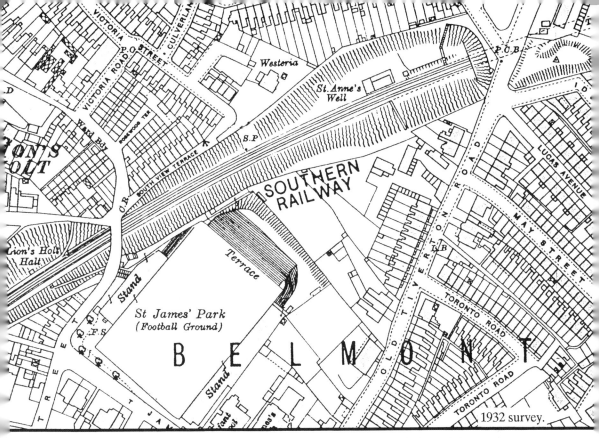

46. Prior to passing through the 263yd long Blackboy Tunnel, the 15.05 Paignton to Exmouth service calls at the short up platform on 10th July 1990. Owing to the limited platform lengths, usually only the branch trains called, almost all of them doing so between 1976 and 1986. East of the tunnel, Mount Pleasant Road Halt was in use from 1906 until 1928. (J.Scrace)

EXMOUTH JUNCTION

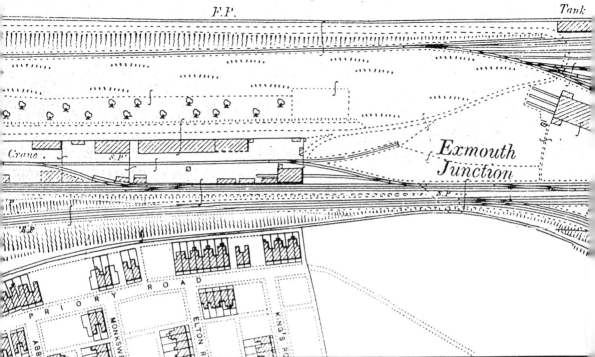

The 1905 survey indicates the extent of the 1887 engine shed. Its steel structure and cladding corroded severely and a replacement was built to the east of it in 1925-27. In 1913 the LSWR established a concrete works on the vacant land shown in the top left part of this map. In 1925-28 the SR greatly expanded the works and the diversity of products. The Exmouth branch is lower right, then single track. The sheds on the left of the map were used by signals and permanent way departments.

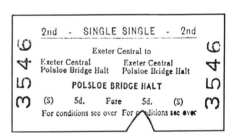

2nd	-	SINGLE SINGLE	-	2nd

Exeter Central to

Exeter Central   Exeter Central
Polsloe Bridge Halt   Polsloe Bridge Halt

POLSLOE BRIDGE HALT

(S)   5d.   Fare   5d.   (S)

For conditions see over   For conditions see over

3546   3546

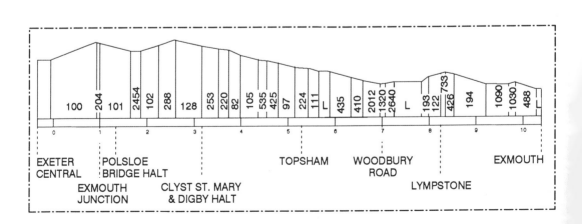

| | 100 | 204 | 101 | 2454 | 102 | 288 | 128 | 253 | 220 | 82 | 105 | 535 | 425 | 97 | 224 | 111 | L | 435 | 410 | 2012 | 1320 | 2640 | L | 193 | 122 | 733 | 426 | 194 | 1090 | 1030 | 488 | L |

EXETER CENTRAL   POLSLOE BRIDGE HALT   TOPSHAM   WOODBURY ROAD   EXMOUTH

EXMOUTH JUNCTION   CLYST ST. MARY & DIGBY HALT   LYMPSTONE

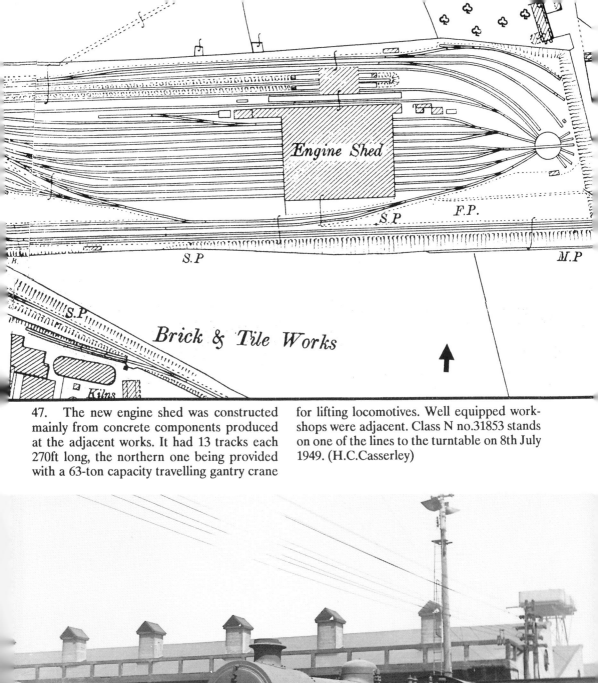

Engine Shed

S.P   F.P.

S.P   M.P.

S.P

Brick & Tile Works

Kilns

47.   The new engine shed was constructed mainly from concrete components produced at the adjacent works. It had 13 tracks each 270ft long, the northern one being provided with a 63-ton capacity travelling gantry crane for lifting locomotives. Well equipped workshops were adjacent. Class N no.31853 stands on one of the lines to the turntable on 8th July 1949. (H.C.Casserley)

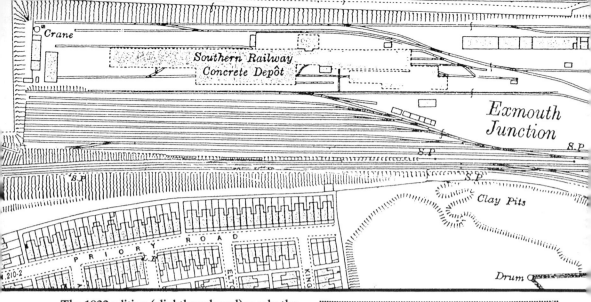

Southern Railway Concrete Depôt

Crane

Exmouth Junction

Clay Pits

Drum

P R I O R Y   R O A D

The 1932 edition (slightly reduced) marks the position of the new electrically-operated 65ft turntable and the 300 ton capacity coaling tower, spanning the tracks to it. Carriage and wagon repair shops were also established on the site. Part of these were in use for civil engineers equipment maintenance in 1991 but the locomotive shed had closed on 6th March 1967. The Concrete Works is upper left, while the Exmouth branch and Polsloe Bridge Halt are lower right. The "brickworks" siding extends south to serve a chemical works, although it is not named as such.

48.   The branch was doubled as far as Topsham on 31st May 1908. Class O2 no.30199 is on the up line on 24th June 1950 outside the brickworks, which had a siding until 12th May 1967. The adjacent chemical works siding was in use from July 1921 until 7th January 1973 and served Collards, later Domestic Chemicals. (J.J.Smith)

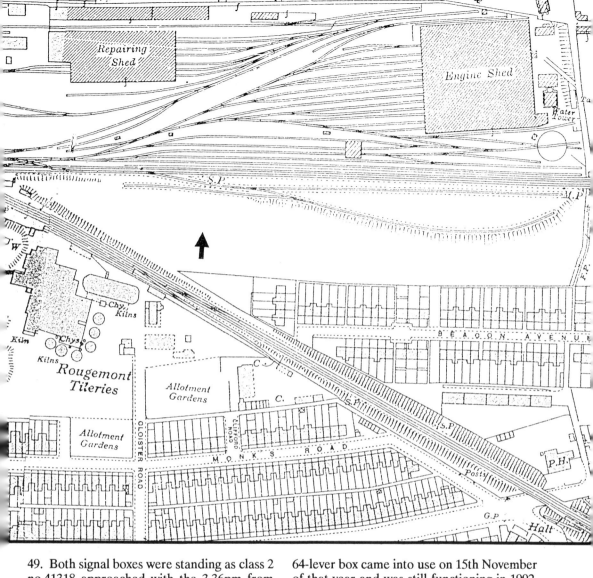

49. Both signal boxes were standing as class 2 no.41318 approached with the 3.36pm from Exmouth on 11th September 1959. The new 64-lever box came into use on 15th November of that year and was still functioning in 1992. (S.P.Derek)

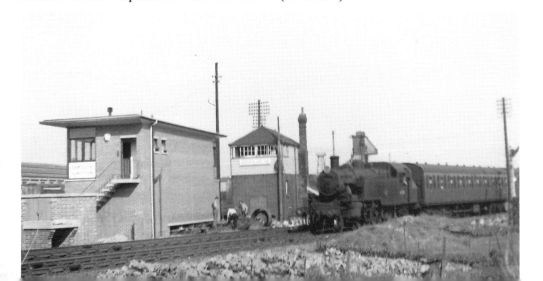

50.   A lower quadrant signal is visible above the rear coach of the class 118 DMU from Exmouth on 15th September 1984. The post for a replacement colour light signal is on the left, the signal being effective from 16th January 1988. Beyond the signal box are the storage bins of the coal concentration depot established on part of the site of the former concrete works on 4th December 1967. (D.Mitchell)

POLSLOE BRIDGE

51. The halt was probably opened on 31st May 1908 when a steam railmotor service commenced between Exeter and Topsham. The 1.25pm Exeter Central-Topsham train is approaching on 24th September 1959, headed by class 3 no.82023. The porch on the ticket office window was then a recent addition. (S.P.Derek)

52. The platforms were rebuilt and extended in 1927 using all concrete components from the nearby works. The fence posts were integral with the slab supports. Even the nameboard was cast in concrete. Exmouth Junction signal box is in the distance as the 11.45am from Exeter Central arrives on 15th September 1963. (C.L.Caddy)

53. Only the up platform remained in use after the track was singled on 4th February 1973. Departing on 5th February 1991 is the 11.15 Exmouth to Barnstaple. The bridge over the stream from which the station probably takes its name is no longer visible, but was near the first oncoming car. The stream passes under the platforms and beyond the tree on the right. (M.Turvey)

SOUTH OF POLSLOE

54. A new bridge was required for the A379 dual carriageway access to the M5. Trains ran over the down line on a temporary bridge for a few months while this concrete structure was completed. The train is the 15.35 from Exeter St.Davids on 5th July 1974. Between 31st May 1908 and 27th September 1948 Clyst St.Mary and Digby Halt had been in use further north (see 1" to 1 mile map in the introduction). Until 10th January 1957, a trailing siding from the up line had been provided to Digby Mental Hospital for its coal supplies. (S.P.Derek)

55. As a wartime measure, sidings were laid on the west side of the line to serve a United States naval store and brought into use on 24th October 1943. However, this prefabricated concrete signal box, which was opened on 23rd January 1944, continued to be used until 3rd February 1973, when the line was singled and it became a ground frame. (C.G.Maggs)

56. This picture and the previous one were taken in 1978. Here we see no.25225 on one of the three sidings in the then UK Naval depot, having worked a trip from Exeter Riverside Yard. Traffic ceased in about 1986. (D.Mitchell)

57. Newcourt Depot and the up line are in the distance as the 14.44 Exeter Central-Exmouth creeps over a temporary bridge on the previously disused down line on 6th April 1975. The new permanent steel span over the M5 had been put in place during the previous weekend. (S.P.Derek)

58. By 23rd July 1975 all was ready for road construction to proceed. The 14.44 service is seen again. The signal is Topsham's down distant. (S.P.Derek)

TOPSHAM

59. The LSWR left its mark on the branch in the form of its architect's Gothic style, Sir William Tite's work surviving at other locations in the district, notably Axminster and Crewkerne. The stone quoins and ornamental ridge tiles help to give distinction to the edifice. (Lens of Sutton)

Trains to Exeter were shown in two different timetables in 1911.

EXETER and TOPSHAM (Motor Cars—1st and 3rd class).—London and South Western.

Miles	Up.	Week Days.														Sundays.							
	Queen Street Sta.,	mrn	mrn	aft	aft	aft	aft	aft	aft	aft						mrn	aft	aft	aft	aft			
	Exeter ¶ ....arr.	8 38	9 55	1230	1 40	2 35	4 3	5 40	7 42	9 40	....	....	....	....	....	10 5	1250	2 15	5 42	8 30	....	....	....
5½	Topsham ....dep.	8 54	1011	1246	1 56	2 51	4 19	5 56	7 58	9 56	....	....	....	....	....	1021	1 6	2 31	5 58	8 46	....	....	....

Miles	Down.	Week Days.														Sundays.							
		mrn	mrn	aft	aft	aft	aft	aft	aft	aft						mrn	aft	aft	aft	aft			
	Topsham ¶ ....dep.	9 18	1038	1 5	2 15	3 2	4 48	6 50	8 3	10 2	....	....	....	....	....	1045	1 25	2 40	6 5	9 0	....	....	....
5½	Exeter (Queen St.) arr.	9 35	1055	1 22	2 32	3 19	5 5	7 7	8 20	1019	....	....	....	....	....	11 2	1 42	2 57	6 22	9 17	....	....	....

¶ "Halts" at Lions Holt, Mount Pleasant Road, Polsloe Bridge, and Clyst St. Mary and Digby, between Exeter (Queen Street) and Topsham.

SIDMOUTH JUNCTION, SIDMOUTH, BUDLEIGH SALTERTON, EXMOUTH, and EXETER.—London and South Western.

Miles	Down.	Week Days.																									Sundays.					
	Waterloo Station,	mrn	mrn	mrn	mrn	mrn	mrn	mrn	mrn	mrn	mrn	mrn	mrn	aft	aft	mrn	mrn	mrn	aft	aft	aft	aft	aft	aft	aft	aft	mrn	aft	aft	aft	aft	
	130London ....dep.	....	....	....	....	....	....	....	....	....	....	....	6 10	....	....	8 50	11 0	....	....	1 0	....	....	3 30	....	....		....	....	....	....	....	....
	133Exeter (Queen St.) "	....	....	....	....	7 20	....	....	....	8 35	....	....	1035	....	....	1 0	....	....	3 25	4 40	....	6 8	6a55	7 40	....		....	....	....	....	....	....
—	Sidmouth Junction ..dep.	....	....	....	....	8 15	....	....	....	9 5	....	....	1110	....	....	1 42	2 10	....	4 5	5 15	....	6 42	7 38	8 20	....	Weds., Fris., and Sats.	....	....	....	....	....	....
2¾	Ottery St. Mary	....	....	....	....	8 24	....	....	....	9 12	....	....	1117	....	....	1 49	2 17	....	4 12	5 22	....	6 51	7 46	8 27	....		....	....	....	....	....	....
5	Tipton St. John's ....arr.	....	7 20	....	....	8 28	....	....	....	9 16	....	....	1121	....	....	1 53	2 21	....	4 16	5 26	....	6 57	7 50	8 31	....		....	....	....	....	....	....
8¼	Sidmouth ....arr.	....	7 30	....	....	8 41	....	....	....	9 28	....	....	1136	....	....	2 6	2 33	....	4 28	5 38	....	7 9	8 3	8 45	....		....	....	....	....	....	....
—	Tipton St. John's ....dep.	....	....	....	....	8 35	....	....	....	9 25	1015	....	1123	....	....	1 59	2 25	....	4 20	5 30	....	7 1	7 56	8 40	....		....	....	....	....	....	....
6¼	Newton Poppleford	....	....	....	....	8 39	....	....	....	9 30	1019	....	1127	....	....	2 3	2 29	....	4 24	5 34	....	7 5	8 0	8 44	....		....	....	....	....	....	....
9¼	East Budleigh	....	....	....	....	8 45	....	....	....	9 37	1025	....	1133	....	....	2 9	2 35	....	4 30	5 40	....	7 11	8 6	8 50	....		....	....	....	....	....	....
11½	Budleigh Salterton......	....	....	....	....	8 50	....	9 10	....	9 47	1031	....	1139	1 0	....	2 14	2 41	....	5 0	5 46	....	7 17	8 12	8 56	9 50		....	....	....	....	....	....
14½	Littleham	....	....	....	....	....	....	9 19	....	9 56	1040	....	1148	1 9	....	2 24	2 50	....	5 10	5 55	....	7 26	8 21	9 5	9 59		....	....	....	....	....	....
16¼	Exmouth .... arr.	....	....	....	....	....	....	9 23	....	10 0	1044	....	1152	1 13	....	2 28	2 54	....	5 14	5 59	....	7 30	8 25	9 9	10 3		....	....	....	....	....	....
	Exmouth .... dep.	6 45	....	7 55	8 25	....	8 55	9 30	9 40	....	1055	1125	1210	1 23	2 15	....	3 35	4 25	5 25	6 5	7 0	7 40	....	9 25	....	1012	9 25	1 0	3 35	5 15	8 10	....
18¼	Lympstone	6 51	...	8 1	8 31	....	9 1	....	9 46	....	11 1	1131	1216	1 29	2 21	....	3 41	4 31	5 31	6 11	7 6	7 46	....	9 31	....	1018	9 31	1 6	3 41	5 21	8 16	....
19¾	Woodbury Road...	6 55	....	8 5	8 35	....	9 5	....	9 50	....	11 5	1135	1220	1 33	2 25	....	3 45	4 35	5 35	6 15	7 10	7 50	....	9 35	....	1022	9 35	1 10	3 45	5 25	8 20	....
21¼	Topsham........(130, 133	6 59	....	8 9	8 39	....	9 9	....	9 54	....	11 9	1139	1224	1 37	2 29	....	3 49	4 39	5 39	6 19	7 14	7 54	....	9 39	....	1026	9 39	1 14	3 49	5 29	8 24	....
26¾	Exeter (Qu.St.) 24, 28, ar	7 10	....	8 20	8 50	....	9 20	9 48	10 5	....	1120	1150	1235	1 48	2 40	....	4 0	4 50	5 50	6 30	7 25	8 5	....	9 50	....	1037	9 50	1 25	4 0	5 40	8 35	....
198¼	133London (Waterloo).arr	11 3	....	....	....	....	....	....	1 47	....	....	3 15	4 38	6 0	....	....	8 7	....	1034	....	3d37	....	....	....	....	....	3 6	7 48	8 30	....	....	....

Miles	Up.	Week Days.																									Sundays.					
	Waterloo Station,	mrn	mrn	mrn	mrn	mrn	mrn	mrn	aft	aft	mrn	mrn	aft	mrn	aft	aft	aft	aft	aft	aft	aft	aft	aft	aft	aft	aft	mrn	aft	aft	aft	aft	
	130London ....dep.	....	....	....	....	....	6 10	....	....	....	8 50	1050	k	1115	....	....	1 0	....	....	....	3 30	....	....	....	5 50	....	....	....	1230	....	4 0	....
—	Exeter (Queen Street) dep.	....	6 55	7 58	9 2	....	1020	1128	....	1245	1 32	2 25	....	3 45	4 33	....	5 30	6 12	6 27	....	7 2	....	8 10	8 45	1015	11 0	1020	2 35	4 35	6 0	8 55	....
5½	Topsham	....	7 8	8 10	9 15	....	1033	1151	....	1258	1 44	2 38	....	3 58	4 46	....	5 43	....	6 40	....	7 15	....	8 23	8 58	1028	1113	1033	2 48	4 48	6 13	9 8	....
7	Woodbury Road..........	....	7 12	8 14	9 19	....	1037	1155	....	1 2	1 48	2 42	....	4 2	4 50	....	5 47	....	6 44	....	7 19	....	8 27	9 2	1032	1117	1037	2 52	4 52	6 17	9 12	....
8¾	Lympstone	....	7 16	8 18	9 23	....	1041	1159	....	1 6	1 52	2 46	....	4 6	4 54	....	5 51	....	6 48	....	7 23	....	8 31	9 6	1036	1121	1041	2 56	4 56	6 21	9 16	....
10½	Exmouth .... arr.	....	7 21	8 23	9 28	....	1046	12 4	....	1 11	1 57	2 51	....	4 11	4 59	....	5 56	6 30	6 53	....	7 28	....	8 36	9 11	1041	1126	1046	3 1	5 1	6 26	9 21	....
	Exmouth .... dep.	6 40	—	8 40	....	9 32	1051	1215	1240	1 18	....	2 56	....	4 20	5 5	....	....	6 35	....	....	7 35	....	....	9 20	....		....	....	....	....	....	....
12¼	Littleham	6 45	Stop	8 45	....	9 37	1056	1220	1245	1 23	....	3 1	....	4 25	5 11	....	....	6 40	....	....	7 40	....	....	9 25	....		....	....	....	....	....	....
15¼	Budleigh Salterton.......	6 55	....	8 55	....	9 46	11 5	1230	1253	1 34	....	3 10	....	4 36	5 19	5 55	....	6 48	....	7 17	7 48	8 15	....	9 33	....	Weds., Fris., and Sats.	....	....	....	....	....	....
17½	East Budleigh	7 1	....	9 0	....	9 51	1110	1235	....	1 39	....	3 15	....	4 41	....	6 0	....	....	....	7 22	....	8 20	....	....	....		....	....	....	....	....	....
20¼	Newton Poppleford.......	7 7	....	9 6	....	9 57	1116	1241	....	1 45	....	3 21	....	4 47	....	6 6	....	....	....	7 28	....	8 26	....	....	....		....	....	....	....	....	....
21¾	Tipton St. John's.....arr.	7 11	mrn	9 10	....	10 1	1120	1245	....	1 49	....	3 25	....	4 51	....	6 10	....	....	....	7 32	....	8 30	....	....	....		....	....	....	....	....	....
—	Sidmouth..........dep.	7 7	7 40	9 5	....	10 0	....	1240	....	....	....	3 20	4 8	4 46	....	6 5	....	....	....	7 27	....	8 25	....	....	....		....	....	....	....	....	....
—	Tipton St. John's.....dep.	7 19	7 50	9 18	....	1011	....	1253	....	....	....	3 31	4 21	4 57	....	6 16	....	....	....	7 38	....	8 36	....	....	....		....	....	....	....	....	....
24	Ottery St. Mary	7 24	7 55	9 23	....	1017	....	1259	....	....	....	3 37	4 27	5 2	....	6 21	....	....	....	7 45	....	8 41	....	....	....		....	....	....	....	....	....
26¾	Sidmouth Jn.130,133 arr	7 32	8 3	9 31	....	1025	....	1 7	....	....	....	3 45	4 35	5 10	....	6 29	....	....	....	7 53	....	8 49	....	....	....		....	....	....	....	....	....
39	130Exeter (Queen St.).arr	8 33	8 33	10 0	....	1132	g	1 53	....	....	....	4 27	5 11	6a0	....	8 1	....	....	....	8a33	....	9 16	....	....	....		....	....	....	....	....	....
186¼	133London (Waterloo) "	11 3	....	....	....	1 47	....	4 38	....	....	....	8 7	....	1034	....	....	....	....	....	3d37	....	....	....	....	....		....	....	....	....	....	....

a Motor Car, 1st and 3rd class. *d* Via Eastleigh. *g* Arrives at 10 50 mrn. on Fridays. *h* Arrives at 9 42 mrn. *i* Arrives at 4 35 aft.
k Not after the 28th instant. *n* Leaves at 11 15 mrn. on and after the 25th instant.

Topsham	1928	1936
No. of passenger tickets issued	87397	51159
No. of season tickets issued	848	973
No. of tickets collected	100595	63984
No. of telegrams	1376	-
Parcels forwarded	5257	3472
Parcels received	3788	4447
Horses forwarded	1	3
General goods forwarded (tons)	2713	1141
General goods received (tons)	2294	1306
Coal, Coke etc.	7661	8026
Other minerals forwarded	5196	3009
Other minerals received	7525	4700
Trucks livestock forwarded	51	4
Trucks livestock received	42	42
Lavatory pennies	648	666

60. A walkway in the "six-foot" and a staff crossing appear in this photograph but in no others that we have seen. Traffic handled by the staff included raspberries, plums, cherries, orchids and salmon! Topsham had a population of around 3000 when its railmotor service to Exeter started in 1908.
(Lens of Sutton)

61. The SR rendered the red brick and stone, removing much of the building's character but presumably reducing water penetration. There is evidence of lengthening of the up platform at both ends. (Lens of Sutton)

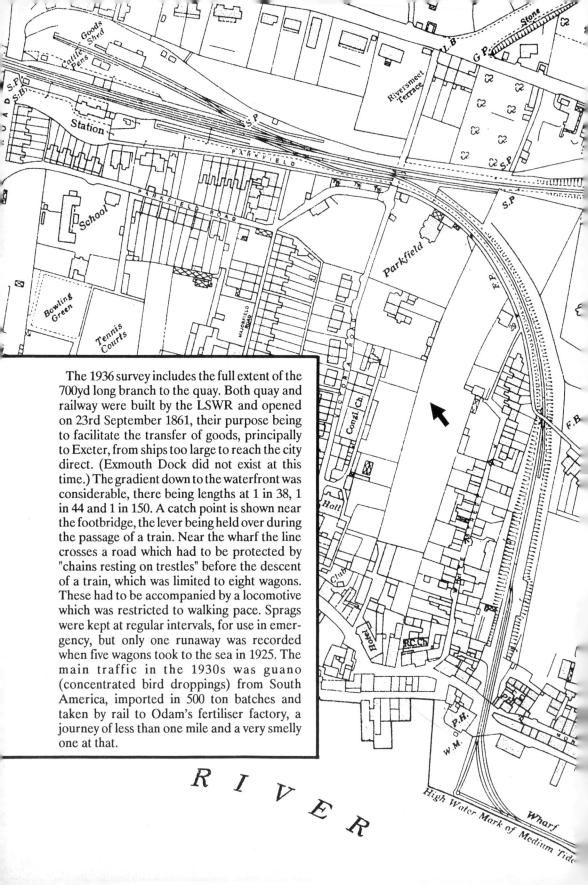

The 1936 survey includes the full extent of the 700yd long branch to the quay. Both quay and railway were built by the LSWR and opened on 23rd September 1861, their purpose being to facilitate the transfer of goods, principally to Exeter, from ships too large to reach the city direct. (Exmouth Dock did not exist at this time.) The gradient down to the waterfront was considerable, there being lengths at 1 in 38, 1 in 44 and 1 in 150. A catch point is shown near the footbridge, the lever being held over during the passage of a train. Near the wharf the line crosses a road which had to be protected by "chains resting on trestles" before the descent of a train, which was limited to eight wagons. These had to be accompanied by a locomotive which was restricted to walking pace. Sprags were kept at regular intervals, for use in emergency, but only one runaway was recorded when five wagons took to the sea in 1925. The main traffic in the 1930s was guano (concentrated bird droppings) from South America, imported in 500 ton batches and taken by rail to Odam's fertiliser factory, a journey of less than one mile and a very smelly one at that.

62. This and the next four pictures were taken on 12th July 1957. Here we are looking up the incline towards the station, the catch point being under the footbridge. The line to the quay closed that year and was lifted in 1958; Holman Way now follows its route. (D.Cullum)

63. Class 3 2-6-2T no.82022 arrives with two ex-LSWR coaches, forming the 1.25pm from Exeter Central, arriving at 1.36. This was the only train of the day to terminate here, returning to Exeter at 1.46, and running Monday to Fridays only. The service was for the benefit of workers returning home for lunch and ceased on 14th June 1963. (D.Cullum)

64. End and side loading docks were provided both sides of the station but cattle pens were only available on the down side. A 2-ton capacity crane was located inside the goods shed, the building surviving for over 20 years after ceasing to serve its intended purpose on 4th December 1968. (D.Cullum)

65. The line to the quay disappears behind the buffers on the right. Until 1908 there was direct access from the down line to the quay and a wagon turntable was provided outside the goods shed. This may have been used for turning early LSWR goods vans, which had a door on one side only. (D.Cullum)

66. Clearly marked 1860, the building survives today, although the fares have increased many times. Younger readers may need to know that the figures refer to shillings/pence - old pence not the present "peas". Staffing ceased on 6th May 1968, the signalmen subsequently being responsible for platform cleaning. (D.Cullum)

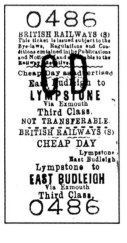

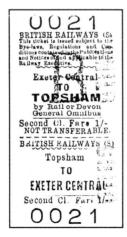

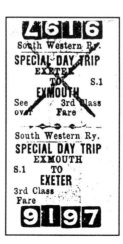

67. The "Birmingham Post Special" on 16th May 1970 was run in connection with the naming of Exmouth's new lifeboat *City of Birmingham*. As Exmouth then lacked run-round facilities and berthing sidings, the train had locomotives each end and departed soon after arrival. It is seen returning to Exeter, forming the 12.45 from Exmouth and carrying a few local passengers. Class 47 no. D1700 is trailing, "Warship" no. D811 being at the front. (S.P.Derek)

68. Signalman Reg Salway leans on the gate wheel which was last used on 20th May 1973, when full lifting barriers were installed. Syke's lock and block was in use to Exmouth Junction until 1959, when it was replaced by BR three-position instruments, which in turn were superseded by the tokenless block system when single line working commenced in 1973. Some of the 23 levers are seen in 1971, the box closing on 30th January 1988, when colour light signals came into use. (S.P.Derek)

SOUTHERN RAILWAY.
RAIL MOTOR CAR.
DAILY WORKMAN
Polsloe Bridge Halt
to Topsham
3rd Class   Fare 5½d
The Passenger is requested to see that
Ticket punched at the time of issue.
Bell Punch Company, London. C842½

Ex   0613

69.   The weed killing train returns from Exmouth on 1st May 1983, with no.47205 leading and no.33042 at the far end. Students of signalling will have noted the unusual combination of upper quadrant arm on a GWR-style post, but may have missed the transposition since picture 67 was taken. Its predecessors are shown in nos. 60 and 63. (D.Mitchell)

70.   The 10.42 from Exeter St.Davids runs in on 5th February 1991, these ageing DMUs having become known as "Heritage units" by then. "EJ" on the post indicates that the passing loop is controlled from Exmouth Junction, as are the lifting barriers. CCTV cameras, on the top of the right post, are used for this purpose. (M.Turvey)

SOUTH OF TOPSHAM

71.   A view south from Elm Grove Road bridge on 2nd August 1985 shows no.45059 at the rear of ten empty coaches from Old Oak Common, bound for Lympstone Commando station, where it would load service personnel travelling on leave to destinations in the North of England. Out of view at the head of the train, no.45063 is entering the Clyst Valley and is about to cross the river. (S.P.Derek)

72.   A heavily loaded relief train passes over the River Clyst on 15th June 1958, headed by class M7 no.30667. At this time the use of the bridge by heavier locomotives was prohibited. Work started on a new bridge twelve months later. (S.C.Nash)

73. The original stone piers were reduced in height to accommodate new steel spans alongside the old bridge, over which class 2 no.41307 is passing with the 11.15am from Exeter Central on 28th January 1960. (S.P.Derek)

74. Class M7 no.30676 creeps over the old bridge on 6th December 1960, while new track is in place on the left. The hand signalman was acting in place of the distant signal, which had been blown down in a gale two days earlier. (S.P.Derek)

75. The new structure came into use on 18th December 1960, the lower level of the piers being evident in this picture taken on 14th May 1961, after loading the ten girders of the old bridge. The Exmouth Junction breakdown crane is being propelled towards Topsham by class 700 0-6-0 no.30691, the engine being obscured by a mess van standing on the adjacent track. Beyond the bridge, the siding to Odam's fertiliser factory trailed off to the left until 1940. It was nearly 500yds long and had a loop near the end. Empty wagons had to travel via Exmouth or be propelled back to Topsham. (S.P.Derek)

EXTON

76. An original postcard shows the name that was in use until 15th September 1958. Woodbury is two miles from the station, whereas Exton is adjacent to it. The proximity of the Exe estuary is evident. The station became "Exton Halt" on 28th February 1965 when it was unstaffed, reverting to "Exton" on 5th May 1969. (D.Cullum coll.)

The 1936 survey reveals the extent of the two sidings which were used for goods traffic until 6th March 1961.

Woodbury Road	1928	1936
No. of passenger tickets issued	15652	7594
No. of season tickets issued	112	1184
No. of tickets collected	21522	8340
No. of telegrams	248	-
Parcels forwarded	930	1245
Parcels received	967	1279
Cans of milk forwarded	972	2715
General goods forwarded (tons)	229	110
General goods received (tons)	704	194
Coal, Coke etc.	598	884
Other minerals forwarded	-	30
Other minerals received	2420	-
Lavatory pennies	-	271

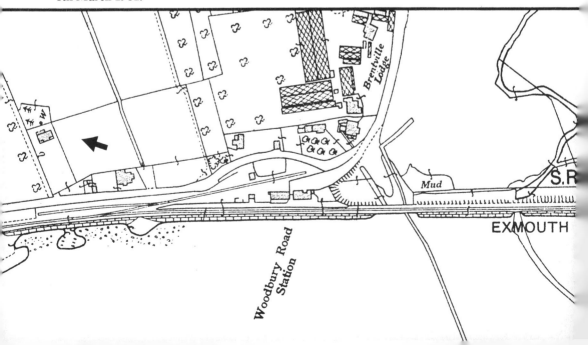

77. The station faces south-west and so a platform canopy would have been of little value in view of the frequency of near horizontal rain from that direction. The signal box is visible but no rodding tunnel can be seen. The box closed on 25th June 1918, when a ground frame was provided. (Lens of Sutton)

78. Camping coach no. 20 was recorded on 29th June 1948, it formerly having been a LSWR lavatory second numbered 599. One of the four lavatories was situated by the word SOUTHERN. All were fitted with tip-up hand basins to save space. (J.H.Aston)

79. Class M7 no. 30323 restarts its train of BR all steel coaches on 23rd May 1957, the station house being visible above the second coach. The bridge on the right passes over a small watercourse, which created a problem three years later, this being illustrated in the picture after next. (T.Wright)

80. Bound for Exeter Central on 15th June 1958 is class 3 no. 82011 with green coaches alternating with red and cream ones. Near the leading axle, a gradient post is indicating the commencement of a climb at only 1 in 2640 up the valley. The rear coach is at the northern extension of the platform. (S.C.Nash)

81. Severe flooding on 3rd October 1960 weakened the bridge adjacent to the station, necessitating immediate temporary repairs. A redundant bridge from Lapford was assembled alongside and is seen on 4th March 1961 as class 3 no. 82010 observes the 5 mph speed limit with the 1.15pm from Exmouth. Two cranes completed the changeover on the following day. (S.P.Derek)

82. Starcross is visible across the Exe as a DMU leaves for Exeter Central in August 1969. The goods yard gate was extant but the sidings had been lifted in 1965, accommodating camping coaches for the last time in the previous summer. (T.Wright)

83. Slowly introduced from the summer of 1990 were the class 155 Sprinters. This one, bound for Exeter, stands at the low platform on 5th February 1991. By then a platform shelter had been provided for passengers and the buildings were becoming a desirable residence. (M.Turvey)

84. A new station was opened on 3rd May 1976 for the exclusive use of the Commando Training Centre Royal Marines, where over 1000 men are usually in barracks. Local trains are much used and leave specials continued to run in 1991, that on 20th December employing nos. 47817 and 37263. (J.Scrace)

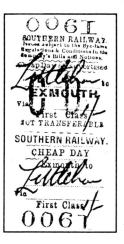

85. Having run parallel to the shore for over two miles, the railway diverges from the water-front shortly before reaching Lympstone. The thatched cottage has long gone. (D.Cullum coll.)

86. The station is approached through a cutting through which class M7 no. 30023 is proceeding with one van and a brake on 25th September 1958. The footbridge was the van-tage point for the previous photograph. The area on the left is now National Trust property. (Pamlin Prints)

LYMPSTONE VILLAGE

87. Unlike Exton, the station faced east and was fairly well sheltered, being partly in a cutting. The goods line was a loop and so could be shunted by trains in either direction. Until WWII large quantities of shellfish were loaded onto passenger trains here.
(Lens of Sutton)

The 1933 edition emphasises the proximity of the station to the village, whose population only increased from about 1100 to 1600 during the first hundred years of the line.

Lympstone	1928	1936
No. of passenger tickets issued	43965	33358
No. of season tickets issued	309	455
No. of tickets collected	55518	45048
No. of telegrams	292	-
Parcels forwarded	939	1122
Parcels received	1032	1758
Cans of milk forwarded	-	4061
Cans of milk received	-	10
General goods forwarded (tons)	128	67
General goods received (tons)	659	248
Coal, Coke etc.	838	676
Other minerals received	143	4
Trucks livestock forwarded	25	2
Trucks livestock received	31	2
Lavatory pennies	228	497

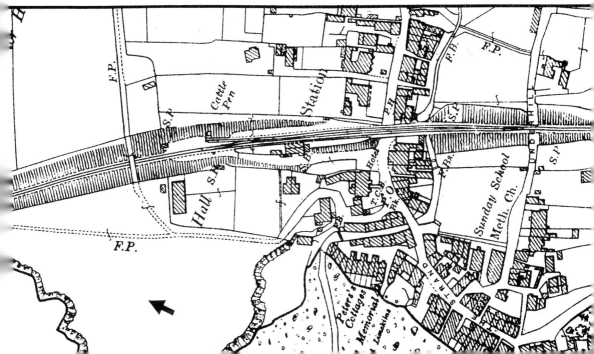

88. The 12.45pm Exeter Central to Exmouth on 31st May 1959 was composed entirely of relatively new BR built stock, although class 2 no. 41306 was of LMS design. The goods loop is on the right, the station being visible at the rear of the train. (S.C.Nash)

89. Adjacent to the station building was the signal box which was in use from 29th September 1929 until 16th September 1962. Its predecessor had been on the opposite side of the goods loop. (S.P.Derek)

90. The fireman of class 3 no. 82013 extends the loop of the tablet pouch as the driver brakes the Exmouth bound train. Access for road vehicles to the goods yard was through the gate on the left and across both the running line and the dock siding - an unusual arrangement. (J.W.T.House/C.L.Caddy)

91. The goods yard was closed on 4th April 1960 but the track remained in place for over two more years. The tail lamp indicates that the DMU is bound for Exmouth. It is about to cross the three-arch brick bridge over the village street in August 1969. (T.Wright)

92. The buildings were demolished in December 1976 but more recently attempts have been made to cheer the site with flower tubs. Despite the destination blind, unit no. 954 was bound for Exmouth on 10th July 1990. The station was renamed Lympstone Village on 13th May 1991. (J.Scrace)

93. Class 142 "Skippers" were in use on the branch from the spring of 1986 to the autum of 1987. Based on National bus components, excessive flange wear proved a problem, this being due to their lack of bogies. By then this fixed distant was the only semaphore signal on the branch. It was removed in January 1988. (S.P.Derek)

Exmouth	1928	1936
No. of passenger tickets issued	181024	116418
No. of season tickets issued	1699	2555
No. of tickets collected	434362	294690
No. of telegrams	3919	2500
Parcels forwarded	8499	6675
Parcels received	36768	3340
Horses forwarded	60	45
Cans of milk forwarded	2	-
Cans of milk received	2623	2771
General goods forwarded (tons)	10572	8111
General goods received (tons)	9018	7328
Coal, Coke etc.	22025	8354
Other minerals forwarded	11459	4390
Other minerals received	5249	359
Trucks livestock received	3	-
Lavatory pennies	37056	36975

The 1890 map shows Warren's siding which was still in place in the 1950s. The works became part of the East Devon Brick & Tile Co.

Exmouth Brick & Tile Works

Mudbank Lane

Sluice

DEVONPORT, TAVISTOCK, OKEHAMPTON, EXMOUTH, BUDLEIGH SALTERTON, SIDMOUTH, SEATON, LYME REGIS, YEOVIL & SALISBURY to LONDON

UP — MONDAYS TO FRIDAYS

		RC am	RC am	RC am	RC am		RC am	RC am	"ATLANTIC COAST EXPRESS" Commences 17th July	R C am		RC am	RC am	RB am	RC pm	RC pm	RC pm
Devonport King's Road	dep	..	..	..	..		8A29	9 0		10A 6		10AC6	11 13	11A50	..	2A29	..	4A 3	..
Tavistock North	„	..	..	..	..	Mondays and Fridays 17th July	9 0	10 40			10C40	11 41	12 25	..	3 0	..	4 31	..
Okehampton	„	..	..	..	..		9 34	11 29			11C29	12 10	1 14	..	3 31	..	5 4	..
Exmouth (via Exeter Central)	„	..	..	..	9 22							12 15		..	3 36	..		..
Exmouth (via Tipton St. John's)	„	..	7 0	..			9A52			11 50			1 29	..		..	5 20	..
Budleigh Salterton	„	..	7 12	..			10A 6			12 4			1 46	..		..	5 32	..
Sidmouth	„	..	7 23	..			9 31	10A20		12 20			2 20	..		..	5 44	..
Seaton	„	6Z 5	7Z20	..			10A 2	10A 2	11 41	11C41			2 30	..	3 46	..	6 10	..
Lyme Regis	„	6Y31	7Y21				9 45	9 45	11 40	11C40		1 8	2 16	..	3 53	..	6 10	..
Pen Mill	„			9 2	9 50									3 53		6 11		..
Yeovil Town	„	7 22	8 20				11 0	11 0	12A35	12AC35		1 50	3 30	..	5 18	..	7 1	..
Yeovil Junction	„	7 31	8 32				11 6	11 6	12 46	12C46		2 5	3 44	..	5 25	..	7 8	..
Salisbury	„	8 27	9 32				12 15	12 32	2 0			2 15	3 15	4 50	..	6 20	..	8 9	..
LONDON Paddington	arr			12 10	1 25										7 10		9 5	..
Waterloo	„	10 8	11 8	..			1 50	2 15	3 32			3 38	5 34	6 33	..	8 6	..	10 8	..

UP — SATURDAYS

		RC am	RC am	RC am	RC am	RB am	am	am	RC am	RC am	RC pm	MB am		RD pm	RC am		RC pm		RC pm
Devonport King's Road	dep	..	..	..	..	..	..	..	8A29	..	..	10 7		..	1113		..		..
Tavistock North	„	..	..	..	..	..	..	..	9 0	..	..	1042		..	1141		..		..
Okehampton	„	..	..	..	..	..	..	..	9 34	1019	1059	1119		..	1211		1257		1 9
Exmouth (via Exeter Central)	„	..	..	..	8 50	..	..	..		1044	1115	1145		..					
Exmouth (via Tipton St. John's)	„	..	7 0	..		..	9A30	..	9 52	1042	..			1214					
Budleigh Salterton	„	..	7 12	..	9A17	..	..	..	10 4	1055	..			1226					
Sidmouth	„	..	7 23	..	9A32	..	..	..	1015	11 7	..			1220					
Seaton	„	6Z 5	7Z20	..	9 15	..	10A20	..	9 11	7 12 5	..								
Lyme Regis	„	6Y31	7 35	..	8 50	..	10A10	..	11 8	..	..	12 10		..	1 14		..		..
Pen Mill	„			9 6	9 50							12 6							
Yeovil Town	„	7 22	8 20	..	10 0	1050	..	1120	1222		..	1 5		..	1 35	1 56	..		..
Yeovil Junction	„	7 31	8 32	..	1019	1058	..	1137	1239		..	1 11		..	1 49	2 6	..		..
Salisbury	„	8 27	9 32	..	1133	1156	12 13	1235	1 34	1 46	..	2 20		..	2 40	3B20	3 30		3 50
LONDON Paddington	arr			1210	1 42						3 30			..					
Waterloo	„	10 9	11 8	..		1 5	1 38	1 57	2 15	3 10	3 23	3 53		..	4 19	5B 4	5 6		5 24

UP — SATURDAYS—continued / SUNDAYS

		RB pm	RB am	RC pm	RC pm		RC pm	RC pm	RC pm	RC pm	am	RC am	RC noon	RC pm	RB pm	RC pm	RC pm	RC pm	RC pm
Devonport King's Road	dep	..	11A50	..	..		2A37	..	4A 3	..	8 33	10A13	..	..	..	..	3A 6	..	..
Tavistock North	„	..	12 37	..	..		3 8	..	4 31	..	9 15	10 44	..	..	..	..	3 39	..	..
Okehampton	„	..	1 17	..	..		3 39	..	5 4	..	9 52	11 15	..	..	..	..	4 9	..	..
Exmouth (via Exeter Central)	„	..	..	2 15	..	2 49	3 36	..	..	..	11 0	12 0	..	..	..	..	4 20	..	5 45
Exmouth (via Tipton St. John's)	„	1A45	..	..	..			..	5 16	..	1035	..	..	3 42	..	..		..	..
Budleigh Salterton	„	2A 4	..	..	..			..	5 28	..	1047	..	..	3 54	..	..		..	..
Sidmouth	„	..	..	2A22	..		2 55	..	5 45	..	11 0	..	1210	..	4 5	..	4 46	..	6 14
Seaton	„	2A35	..	..	..		3 47	..	6 10	..	1132	..	..	3 52	..	..	5 10	..	6 33
Lyme Regis	„	..	..	3A 5	..			5 40	6 12	..	1134	..	..	3 0	..	..	5 10	..	..
Pen Mill	„	..	..	..	3 53									4 12		5	..	5 55	..
Yeovil Town	„	..	3 30	..	..		5 18	..	7 17	10	1235	1 2	..	5 10	..	5	6 0	..	7 35
Yeovil Junction	„	..	3 47	..	..		5 25	..	7 8	7 20	1243	1 9	..	5 18	..	..	6 10	..	7 42
Salisbury	„	4 30	4 44	4 57	..	5 5	5 36	6 20	..	8 9	8 30	1 33	1 58	2 23	..	6 18	..	7 15	..	8 32
LONDON Paddington	arr				7 15				9 5	..					7 45	..	8 30		9 25	..
Waterloo	„	6 13	6 19	6 41	..		7 36	8 10	..	10 8	11 13	7 3	49	4 14	..	7 49	..	9 15	..	1021

A Seats may be reserved at a fee of 2/- per seat, upon personal or postal request to the Station Master. Early application is advisable.

B Dep Salisbury 3 40 pm and arr Waterloo 5 15 pm until 8th July, also 9th September

C Applies until 14th July

MB Miniature Buffer Car for whole or part of journey

RB Buffet Car for whole or part of journey

RC Restaurant Car for whole or part of journey

RD Restaurant Car provided 1st July to 19th August

Y By Southern National Omnibus between Lyme Regis and Axminster. Times subject to alteration

Z By Southern or Western National Omnibus to Axminster Station. Times subject to alteration

Summary of principal services for June to September 1961. The corresponding table for down trains can be found opposite picture 113 in *Branch Lines to Seaton and Sidmouth*.

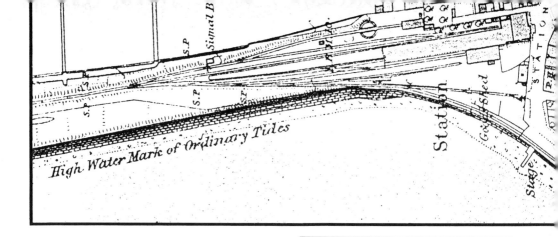

EXMOUTH

The 1890 edition shows the presence of a turntable and the full extent of the branch to Exmouth Dock. The turntable was installed in 1862 and was removed in 1927, having been out of use for many years.

The Illustrated London News included this drawing of the opening ceremony which took place on 1st May 1861. The second train (8.16am from Exeter) was reported to have had nineteen coaches and two engines, as seen here. The engine shed is on the left and the goods shed on the right.
(Devon County Libraries)

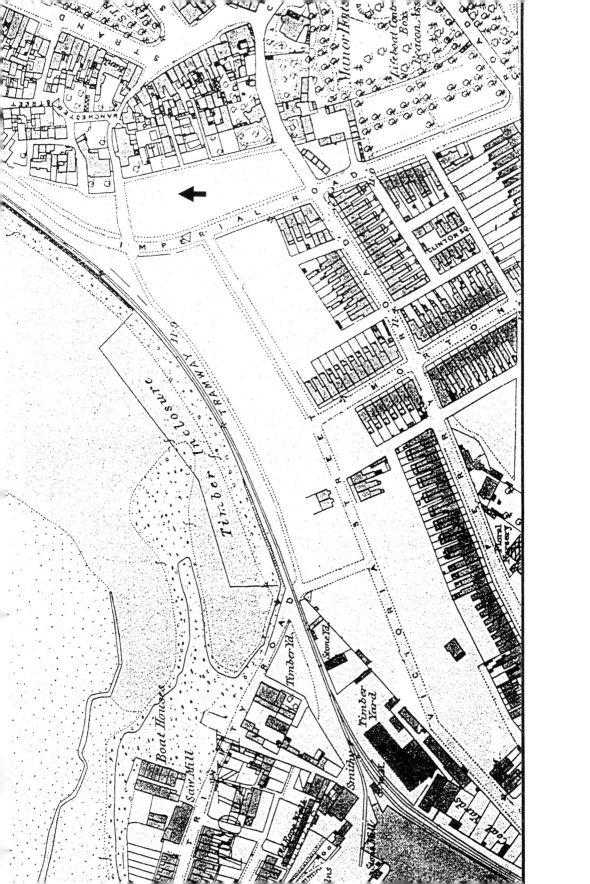

94. Notes with this photograph of the original terminus state that it was in Imperial Road (later Station Parade) and that what appears to be an incomplete footbridge over the dock tramway, near the landing stage, was "a high platform from which height Exmouth pilots looked out to sea". The horse is standing near the entrance to the goods yard.
(Devon County Library)

95. A view in the opposite direction along Station Parade in January 1924 has the terminal building in the centre. The new terminus is under constructon behind it, the builder's scaffold poles being visible. The old building was demolished to make way for a spacious forecourt. The building on the left was railway property and probably included stables. (C.G.Maggs coll.)

96. The new station, which opened on 20th July 1924, is seen on 18th June 1926, along with the old water tank for locomotive supply. The short train is bound for Tipton St. Johns behind the gleaming class O2, no. E 187. (H.C.Casserley)

97. The fireman trims the coal before departing for Exeter on 27th September 1947. The population was considerable at about 6000 when the line opened. By 1931 it was about 14,000, this figure doubling 50 years later. (J.H.Aston)

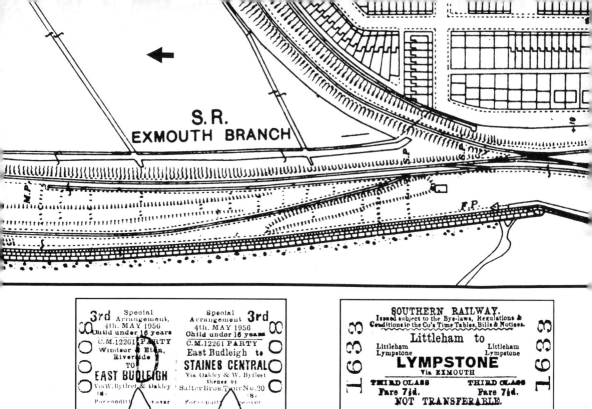

S. R.
EXMOUTH BRANCH

98. Only three members of the once numerous 0415 class survived WWII and were used almost exclusively on the Lyme Regis branch. No. 30583 was running round an enthusiasts' railtour when photographed on 12th April 1953. It had run direct from Exeter and was to return via Sidmouth Junction. The locomotive had been on the East Kent Railway from 1919 until 1946 and is now on the Bluebell Railway. (N.Sprinks)

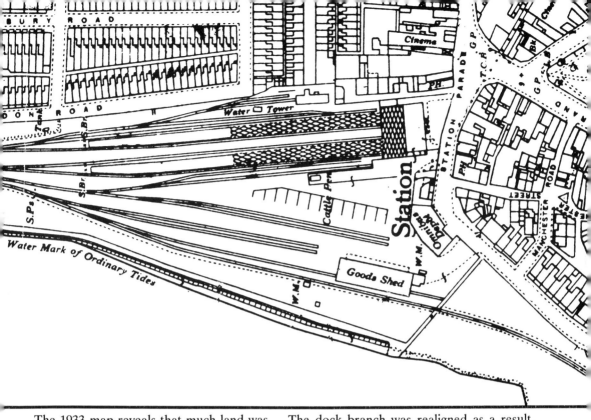

The 1933 map reveals that much land was reclaimed from the sea by 1924, so that the yard could be enlarged and a new goods shed built.

99. Although modern locomotives were sent to work the branch from 1952 onwards, they were often coupled to elderly coaches. Class

The dock branch was realigned as a result. Top left is the line to Tipton St. Johns.

3 no. 82017 is departing at 5.15pm, bound for Exeter with five ex-LSWR vehicles on 30th August 1954. (J.N.Faulkner)

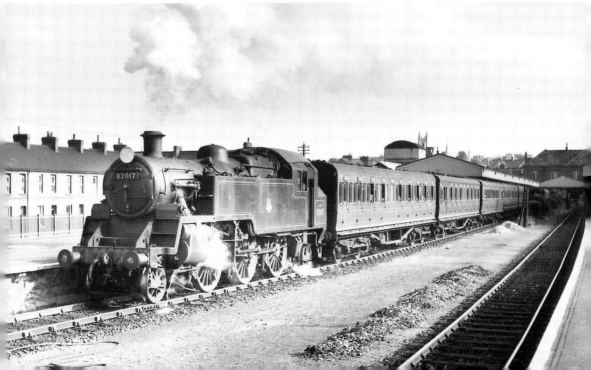

Spend Saturday by the Sea

AND

DANCE AT THE PAVILION

EXMOUTH from 7.30 to 11.30

The Management of **The Pavilion, Exmouth** by arrangement and with the co-operation of **British Railways** (Southern Region) offer for the convenience of the Public, and **PARTICULARLY THOSE WHO WISH TO TAKE ADVANTAGE OF DANCING IN EXMOUTH'S SEA-FRONT PAVILION BALLROOM,** a **LATE TRAIN** to Exeter (calling at stations en route) **EACH SATURDAY AND BANK HOLIDAY** until further notice and commencing on **Saturday, 1st May, 1948**

TIME TABLE

Depart	EXMOUTH	11.45 p.m.
Arrive	Lympstone	11.50 p.m.
,,	Woodbury Road	11.55 p.m.
,,	Topsham	12.00
,,	Polsloe Bridge Halt	12.10 a.m.
,,	EXETER CENTRAL	12.15 a.m.

Return Fare (from Exeter) 3/1 2/4

A Cheap Daily Return will be issued at a later date

A Reduction to Patrons of the Pavilion on 3/- admission will be given upon production of return half of rail ticket

100. The original wooden engine shed was replaced by this 70ft long concrete structure in 1927. Photographed in about 1956, there was normally an allocation of four engines at the shed. Note that the engines face the up direction, this being a general rule at this shed. (J.W.T.House/C.L.Caddy)

101. On 24th May 1957, class O2 no. 30199 was involved in carriage shunting. Also included in this view is the 5-ton capacity gantry or portal crane and the massive goods shed, beyond which passes the dock branch. The shed was later used for skate boarding and now forms part of a sports complex. (T.Wright)

102. The signalman's view shows that platform 4 (left) has an engine release road, as has platform 1. These were generally used for arrivals and nos. 2 and 3 for departures. (R.C.Riley)

BRITISH RAILWAYS (S)

EXCESS TICKET

Issued at Exmouth

in conjunction with Return Half of

1st. CLASS ORDINARY RETURN

No. ....

Permitting travel via Exeter

First Class. Fare 1/5H

0140   0140

SOUTHERN RAILWAY.

EXCESS TICKET

Issued at Exmouth

in conjunction with Return Half of

Third Class

MONTHLY or TOURIST ticket.

No. ....

Permitting travel via Exeter.

xcess Fare 6d

3756   3756

103. The imposing facade was recorded on 12th July 1957, before the town became over-crowded with motor traffic and the consequent white lines, yellow lines etc. In early 1969, the building was vacated and let out as shops, a ticket kiosk being provided on the remaining platform. Access was through a passage near the telephone box. (D.Cullum)

104. Class M7 no. 30676 is propelling stock into platform 2 on 12th October 1959 prior to departure for Tipton St. Johns. Platforms 3 and 4 were normally used for these services as this avoided conflicting with Exeter trains. Holiday traffic was once very heavy - for example 18,500 people booked to Exmouth from Waterloo in 1936. (R.C.Riley)

105. The signalman is on his balcony with the single line tablet as class 3 no. 82017 leaves for Exeter on the same day. The Tipton St. Johns route curves sharply at 20 chains radius beyond the box. The climb behind the house was at 1 in 50 for one mile to Littleham. (R.C.Riley)

106. The signalman waits on the outer end of the balcony for the tablet from the crew of class 2 no. 41318 as it arrives from Exeter. This class of locomotive was introduced to the branch in July 1952. (R.C.Riley)

107. One of the popular Lyme Regis locomotives was used on 11th March 1961 with the Westward TV exhibition train. This is no. 30582 which was built by Stephensons in 1885. It was maintained at Exmouth Junction and was scrapped in 1962. (S.C.Nash)

108. The Western Region, having taken over on 1st January 1963, soon explored ways of making economies in operation. Here we witness the first trial of a DMU on the branch on 12th June 1963. One problem was that the tablet exchange had to take place with the unit almost stationary and the signalman had to descend to ground level. (S.P.Derek)

109. The circulating area and the little used water columns were recorded in October 1963. The plants between the tracks included palms, no doubt intended to impress travellers with the suitability of the local climate for holidays. (Wessex coll.)

110. DMUs operated most Exeter services from September 1963, the locomotive shed closing officially on 8th November of that year. One of the new units waits to form the 13.45 to Sidmouth Junction on 14th September 1966. The shed, with its integral water tank, was demolished in 1967. (J.M.Tolson/F.Hornby)

SOUTHERN RAILWAY.
This ticket is issued subject to the Company's Bye-laws, Regulations and Conditions in their Time Tables, Notices and Book of Regulations. Available on DAY of issue ONLY.
Exmouth to
Exmouth   Exmouth
Budleigh S.   Budleigh S.
BUDLEIGH SALTERTON
Via LITTLEHAM
Third Class   Third Class
Fare 7½d   Fare 7½d

6158   6158

111. The new 70-lever signal box came into use in 1924 and is seen on 4th March 1967, manned by Reg Salway. Closure took place on 10th March 1968, after which time a single wooden train staff was in use between here and Topsham. (S.P.Derek)

112. This ex-US Army recovery vehicle was used to move track materials from the Budleigh Salterton line and is seen on the former engine shed road on 31st August 1968. A DMU is in no. 2 platform but after 20th December of that year, only no. 4 was used. (S.P.Derek)

→

113. In August 1969, the cutters were at work in the yard as an Exeter train departed from platform 4, passed under the armless signal gantry and in front of the deserted box. (T.Wright)

→

114. The site was returning to nature when a charter train from South Wales arrived on 15th August 1971, with "Warship" no. 814 at the far end. Nearest is Brush type 4 no. 1609. In 1984, a traffic survey revealed the following percentages - commuters 30, shoppers 19, scholars 15 and passengers continuing to InterCity services 25. (D.Mitchell)

115. In 1975, work commenced on a new transport interchange in which the old platform 2 would be served by a new terminal building. White pegs indicate the proposed position of the track. Sadly the palm was not retained. (S.P.Derek)

116. The new station came into use on 2nd May 1976 when the single line was slewed over from the former no. 4 platform. The old buildings were demolished prior to road construction work in 1980. Marine Way was opened on the site of the former platforms 3 and 4 on 10th December 1981. (J.Scrace)

EXMOUTH DOCK

The 1933 map shows the limited size of the dock, which opened in 1868 and could take ships of up to 750 tons. Most traffic was inwards, notably coal for local consumption and herrings, which were sent by rail to London for many years. The coal gantry is evident in the photographs.

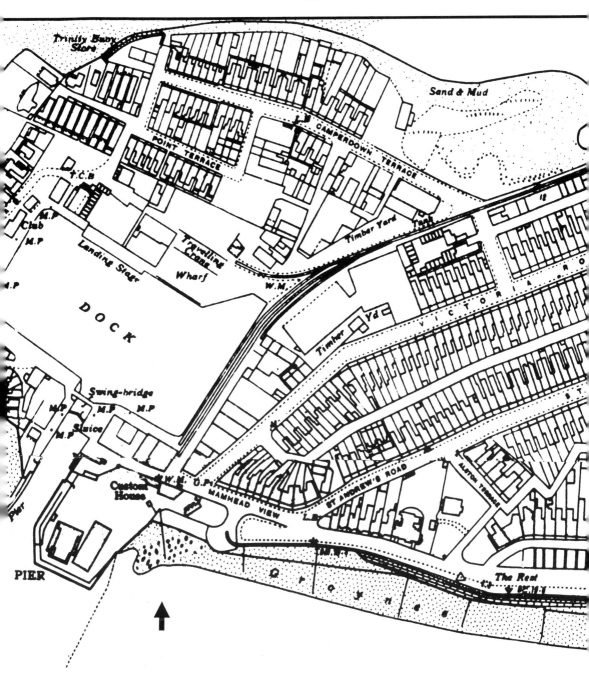

117. The branch commenced by the goods shed (centre) and immediately passed over the lane to the playing fields, the crossing gates being visible. A coach in a siding can be seen between the two buses. (Pamlin Prints)

118. All wagons had to be propelled to the dock, as no loop was provided. Class 2 no. 41307 is doing so on 24th September 1958, having just passed over Camperdown Terrace where a flagman would have been present. (Pamlin Prints)

119. On reaching the dock, drivers were confronted with a splay of five sidings, more than shown on the 1933 map. Only class O2 and BR class 2 locomotives were allowed on the branch, owing to a restriction on the weighbridge by the goods shed. Imported timber, fertiliser and apples (for Whiteways at Whimple) have been other important traffic. (Pamlin Prints)

120. A final view from 1958 shows one of the popular features of glorious Devon - the busy waterfront. The private siding agreement terminated in December 1967 but the dock continued in use for commercial shipping until December 1990. (Pamlin Prints)

MP Middleton Press

Easebourne Lane, Midhurst. West Sussex. GU29 9AZ
Tel: (0730) 813169   Fax: (0730) 812601
Write or telephone for our latest booklist

BRANCH LINES

BRANCH LINES TO MIDHURST
BRANCH LINES AROUND MIDHURST
BRANCH LINES TO HORSHAM
BRANCH LINE TO SELSEY
BRANCH LINES TO EAST GRINSTEAD
BRANCH LINES TO ALTON
BRANCH LINE TO TENTERDEN
BRANCH LINES TO NEWPORT
BRANCH LINES TO TUNBRIDGE WELLS
BRANCH LINE TO SWANAGE
BRANCH LINE TO LYME REGIS
BRANCH LINE TO FAIRFORD
BRANCH LINE TO ALLHALLOWS
BRANCH LINES AROUND ASCOT
BRANCH LINES AROUND WEYMOUTH
BRANCH LINE TO HAWKHURST
BRANCH LINES AROUND EFFINGHAM JN
BRANCH LINE TO MINEHEAD
BRANCH LINE TO SHREWSBURY
BRANCH LINES AROUND HUNTINGDON
BRANCH LINES TO SEATON AND SIDMOUTH
BRANCH LINES AROUND WIMBORNE

SOUTH COAST RAILWAYS

CHICHESTER TO PORTSMOUTH
BRIGHTON TO EASTBOURNE
RYDE TO VENTNOR
EASTBOURNE TO HASTINGS
PORTSMOUTH TO SOUTHAMPTON
HASTINGS TO ASHFORD
SOUTHAMPTON TO BOURNEMOUTH
ASHFORD TO DOVER
BOURNEMOUTH TO WEYMOUTH
DOVER TO RAMSGATE

SOUTHERN MAIN LINES

HAYWARDS HEATH TO SEAFORD
EPSOM TO HORSHAM
CRAWLEY TO LITTLEHAMPTON
THREE BRIDGES TO BRIGHTON
WATERLOO TO WOKING
VICTORIA TO EAST CROYDON
EAST CROYDON TO THREE BRIDGES
WOKING TO SOUTHAMPTON
WATERLOO TO WINDSOR
LONDON BRIDGE TO EAST CROYDON
BASINGSTOKE TO SALISBURY
SITTINGBOURNE TO RAMSGATE
YEOVIL TO EXETER
CHARING CROSS TO ORPINGTON
VICTORIA TO BROMLEY SOUTH

COUNTRY RAILWAY ROUTES

BOURNEMOUTH TO EVERCREECH JN
READING TO GUILDFORD
WOKING TO ALTON
BATH TO EVERCREECH JUNCTION
GUILDFORD TO REDHILL
EAST KENT LIGHT RAILWAY
FAREHAM TO SALISBURY
BURNHAM TO EVERCREECH JUNCTION
REDHILL TO ASHFORD
YEOVIL TO DORCHESTER
ANDOVER TO SOUTHAMPTON

LONDON SUBURBAN RAILWAYS

CHARING CROSS TO DARTFORD
HOLBORN VIADUCT TO LEWISHAM
KINGSTON & HOUNSLOW LOOPS
CRYSTAL PALACE AND CATFORD LOOP
LEWISHAM TO DARTFORD
MITCHAM JUNCTION LINES

STEAMING THROUGH

STEAMING THROUGH EAST HANTS
STEAMING THROUGH SURREY
STEAMING THROUGH WEST SUSSEX
STEAMING THROUGH THE ISLE OF WIGHT
STEAMING THROUGH WEST HANTS

OTHER RAILWAY BOOKS

GARRAWAY FATHER & SON
LONDON CHATHAM & DOVER RAILWAY
INDUSTRIAL RAILWAYS OF THE S. EAST
WEST SUSSEX RAILWAYS IN THE 1980s
SOUTH EASTERN RAILWAY

OTHER BOOKS

WALKS IN THE WESTERN HIGH WEALD
TILLINGBOURNE BUS STORY
MILITARY DEFENCE OF WEST SUSSEX
BATTLE OVER SUSSEX 1940
SURREY WATERWAYS
KENT AND EAST SUSSEX WATERWAYS
HAMPSHIRE WATERWAYS